Electronic Spies

Other Publications:

HOW THINGS WORK
WINGS OF WAR
CREATIVE EVERYDAY COOKING
COLLECTOR'S LIBRARY OF THE UNKNOWN
CLASSICS OF WORLD WAR II
TIME-LIFE LIBRARY OF CURIOUS AND UNUSUAL FACTS
AMERICAN COUNTRY
VOYAGE THROUGH THE UNIVERSE
THE THIRD REICH
THE TIME-LIFE GARDENER'S GUIDE
MYSTERIES OF THE UNKNOWN
TIME FRAME
FIX IT YOURSELF
FITNESS, HEALTH & NUTRITION
SUCCESSFUL PARENTING
HEALTHY HOME COOKING
UNDERSTANDING COMPUTERS
LIBRARY OF NATIONS
THE ENCHANTED WORLD
THE KODAK LIBRARY OF CREATIVE PHOTOGRAPHY
GREAT MEALS IN MINUTES
THE CIVIL WAR
PLANET EARTH
COLLECTOR'S LIBRARY OF THE CIVIL WAR
THE EPIC OF FLIGHT
THE GOOD COOK
WORLD WAR II
HOME REPAIR AND IMPROVEMENT
THE OLD WEST

For information on and a full description of
any of the Time-Life Books series listed above,
please call 1-800-621-7026 or write:
Reader Information
Time-Life Customer Service
P.O. Box C-32068
Richmond, Virginia 23261-2068

THE NEW FACE OF WAR

Electronic Spies

BY THE EDITORS OF
TIME-LIFE BOOKS, ALEXANDRIA, VIRGINIA

CONSULTANTS

WILLIAM E. BURROWS has written extensively about the collection of intelligence data from aircraft and satellites. He currently teaches at New York University, where he is director of the science and environmental reporting program.

COLONEL RICHARD H. GRAHAM (Ret.) flew SR-71s beginning in the mid-1970s. In the 1980s he became a Squadron Commander, and then Wing Commander of the Ninth Strategic Reconnaissance Wing.

ROBERT H. HOPKINS III is a retired Air Force pilot, most recently an RC-135 aircraft commander during Operation Desert Storm in 1991. An authority on reconnaissance aircraft, he is editor of *The Journal of Military Aviation*.

WILLIAM T. K. JOHNSON specializes in synthetic-aperture radar systems at the Jet Propulsion Laboratory, where he has worked since 1975. He is currently Radar Systems Chief Engineer for the Magellan Mission, which obtains radar images of the surface of Venus.

COLONEL RODERICK J. LENAHAN (Ret.) has been involved with many facets of intelligence collection, analysis, mission planning, and support. He retired in 1988 as chief of intelligence for the Air Force Special Operations Command.

JEFFREY RICHELSON has written numerous books and articles on intelligence and military space operations. He has also taught at several universities.

BEN R. RICH, former president of the Lockheed Advanced Development Company, also known as the Skunk Works, joined Lockheed in 1950. He participated in the design aspects of the F-104, U-2, YF-12, and SR-71.

COLONEL T. C. SKANCHY, recently retired from the U.S. Air Force, commanded a fighter wing and the F-15 Division, Fighter Weapons School at Nellis Air Force Base, Nevada. He also served there as the vice commander of Red Flag, the Air Force's combined air operations training program.

LAWRENCE SULC worked for more than two decades as an operations officer with the Central Intelligence Agency, mostly overseas. He is now president of the Nathan Hale Institute and consults on intelligence, counterterrorism, and security matters.

CONTENTS

The Satellite's Prying Eye

When the thunder of war bursts upon today's world, some of the most valuable military tools perform their jobs in utter silence: Hundreds or thousands of miles above the earth, satellites watch and listen as they make orbital passes over the battleground or hover in a fixed spot by matching the planet's rotation. The robotic observers not only take pictures, but they also eavesdrop on radio communications, probe through clouds with radar, and monitor emanations of heat, tattletale of missile launches and many other phenomena of battle.

Spying from space got its start in 1960 with a 300-pound U.S. satellite that took photographs of the interior of the Soviet Union, then returned from orbit with exposed rolls of film for a parachute descent to a recovery plane waiting below. Since then, satellites have acquired far sharper senses, shifted to electronic imaging systems, and in some cases gained the ability to maneuver close to trouble spots. Such improvements enabled them to play a vital role in conflicts ranging from the Falklands Islands to Afghanistan, but their finest hour came after Saddam Hussein invaded Kuwait in August 1990. For images alone, a half-dozen military satellites were mustered to serve coalition forces during Operation Desert Storm. Their output remains classified, but commanders also used publicly available pictures from commercial satellites. As seen here and on the following pages, even those lower-resolution views were rich in the sort of reconnaissance detail that has revolutionized war.

APPLE OF SADDAM'S EYE. Lacking an up-to-date plan of Kuwait City as war loomed after Iraq's seizure of Kuwait, coalition forces found a quick substitute in the output of commercial satellites ordinarily devoted to work in such fields as land management and urban planning. This portrait of the Kuwaiti capital and environs was created by using computers to blend data from two such satellites, the U.S. Landsat system and France's SPOT, a French acronym for earth-observation satellite. Intended as a general overview, the scene shows objects down to the size of about thirty feet—as compared to a few inches for some military satellites.

7

A SOVIET VIEW. Commercial satellite imagery is available from the Russians as well as from the Western powers. This picture, recorded in September 1990 by a Cosmos satellite, embraces much of northeastern Saudi Arabia, including the air base at Dhahran *(below)*.

AN ACCRETION OF MIGHT. A detail of the Soviet image reveals part of the coalition buildup at Dhahran, 160 miles south of the Kuwaiti border. Nearly thirty jet fighters are parked on the tarmac in a long, broken line; darker aircraft shapes nearby belong to transports ranging in size up to the giant C-5, largest in the American inventory. Because the picture is a photograph rather than a digital image—standard with Western satellites—it cannot be enhanced by computers. Even so, such a view could have helped the Iraqis, but there is no evidence that the Soviets shared satellite pictures with them.

VAGUE FEATURES IN THE DESERT. Taken from an altitude of about 500 miles by a French SPOT satellite, this image covers a 1,400-square-mile area of southeastern Iraq, including an airfield *(upper left)* on the outskirts of the city of Basra.

A POTENTIAL THREAT. Enlarging a portion of the SPOT image discloses the presence of a surface-to-air missile site about twenty-five miles outside Basra. Before the air campaign began, coalition planners purchased more than a hundred of the wideview SPOT pictures to supplement the narrow-view pictures taken by military satellites. The French satellites take black-and-white pictures both in the visible spectrum and in narrow bands outside it to emphasize different features of the world below. Adjustable viewing angles allow scrutiny of any location within a 600-mile-wide corridor.

THE IRAQI SEAT OF POWER. In a forty-by-forty-mile SPOT view taken on February 17, 1991, the Tigris River meanders through Baghdad. Mission planners used such expansive images to familiarize pilots with the geography of a target area and show the best routes in and out.

BROKEN LINKS ACROSS A RIVER. In this detail of the SPOT picture at left, a pair of bridges spanning the Tigris River in a residential area of Baghdad lie broken by laser-guided bombs. Mission planners depended heavily on satellite imagery—including radar views taken through cloud cover or smoke by the ultrasophisticated U.S. Lacrosse satellite—to assess bomb damage and determine whether additional air strikes would be necessary. A month after this picture was recorded on March 10, 1991, the conflict officially ended with a United Nations-sponsored cease-fire.

Getting the Goods on Qadafi

Tracers spray the night sky over Tripoli as Libyan antiaircraft gunners blindly chase after U.S. planes retaliating for the bombing of a Berlin discotheque that killed two American soldiers. Heavy electronic jamming and the threat of deadly U.S. antiradar missiles largely deprived air defenses of radar guidance. Rendered ineffective, they accounted for no aircraft losses.

Late on April 4, 1986, at a dinner party in West Berlin, Brigadier General Thomas Griffin, commander of U.S. Army forces in the city, was told about an ominous scrap of hot intelligence. Earlier that evening, British intelligence operatives at a secret listening post, working in close cooperation with American security agents, had intercepted and decoded a cable to Tripoli, the capital of Libya, from its embassy in East Berlin. "We have something planned that will make you happy," said the dispatch. "It will happen soon. The bomb will blow. American soldiers must be hit."

General Griffin had reason to believe that the message represented a credible threat to his troops. In recent weeks, there had been a marked increase in tensions between Libya and the United States, which had long opposed Libyan strongman Muammar al-Qadafi for his efforts to destabilize neighboring African states and promote international terrorism. More than once, Qadafi had threatened reprisals against U.S. citizens and high officials, including the chief executive. In 1981, after two Libyan jets were downed by Navy F-14s in a dogfight over the Gulf of Sidra—which Qadafi claimed as a Libyan lake and the United States saw as international waters— the dictator had vowed in a telephone conversation to assassinate President Ronald Reagan. He had been overheard by the National Security Agency (NSA), the branch of the U.S. espionage apparatus charged with intercepting communications around the world. Secret Service agents guarding the president were put on top alert, and reports circulated that Libyan hit men had actually entered the United States. The mere threat of such an intrusion—none was ever documented—was enough to make Qadafi and his agents prime targets of U.S. intelligence agencies.

In January of 1986, circumstantial evidence surfaced linking Libya to a bloody assault at the Rome airport by terrorists wielding hand grenades and automatics—an attack that left seventeen people dead, five of them Americans. Although Reagan ruled out re-

15

taliation at the time (the evidence of the Libyan connection was too circumstantial to support punitive action), he became determined to diminish Qadafi at the first opportunity. He asked that efforts be redoubled to find proof of Libyan involvement in a terrorist act.

On March 24, when elements of a U.S. carrier battle group entered the Gulf of Sidra in the ongoing effort to establish the right of American ships to sail there, two Libyan patrol boats armed with antiship missiles approached. Considering them a threat because of Qadafi's promises to attack any U.S. vessel entering the gulf and the launching earlier that day of surface-to-air missiles at Navy fighters, the task force commander sent A-6s from the carriers *Saratoga* and *America.* They sank one patrol boat and damaged the other.

This time, Qadafi's response was unmistakable. On March 25, the NSA intercepted messages from Tripoli to Libyan embassies in thirty nations calling for raids on prominent U.S. targets. Several such assaults were carried out or attempted in the next few days, in Greece, Lebanon, and Bolivia. Then, on April 2, after uncovering a plot by two of Qadafi's diplomats to mount an attack on the U.S. visa office in Paris, French authorities began expelling members of the Libyan diplomatic mission.

Because of this background of violence, General Griffin reacted quickly, dispatching teams of

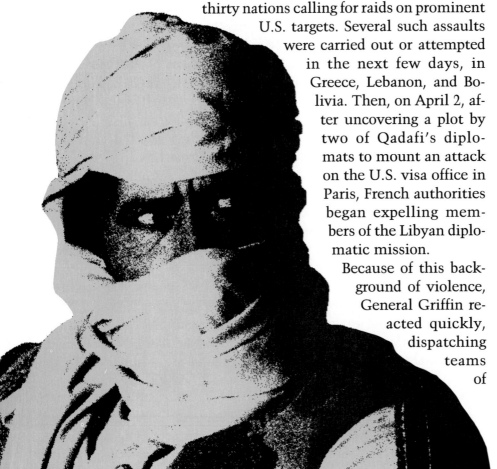

Headdress arranged to reveal only his eyes, Colonel Muammar al-Qadafi saw himself as the embodiment of militant Arab nationalism. Long suspected of sponsoring international terrorism, the Libyan strongman overplayed his hand in 1986 when American and British intelligence collectors implicated him in the bombing of the La Belle discotheque.

16

military policemen to check out the most vulnerable targets—the various bars in West Berlin that U.S. troops frequented. It was a Friday night, and the many soldiers out on the town had dozens of nightspots to choose from. Just before 2:00 a.m., MPs were on their way to one of the GI hangouts, the La Belle discotheque, when a blast ripped through the building. One U.S. serviceman and a Turkish woman accompanying him were killed on the spot. Another GI was mortally wounded, and more than 200 of the 500 soldiers and civilians jammed into the disco at the time were injured. Within minutes of the explosion, the embassy in East Berlin transmitted a message to Tripoli announcing that the operation had succeeded and that no one would be able to trace the deed to Libya.

Communications intelligence—known in the trade as comint—had furnished President Reagan and his aides with what they called the "smoking gun"—documentation of Libyan complicity in a terrorist act. This all-but-conclusive evidence caused a stir at high levels in Washington. Within days, President Reagan ordered preparations for a retaliatory strike, and U.S. officials began hinting at the existence of the intercepts with the object of muting the international outcry that would surely follow any American reprisal.

These public disclosures of top-secret information worried members of the intelligence community, who realized that Libya would respond to the revelation that its diplomatic codes had been broken by switching to alternative ciphers. "The leaks have caused us a setback," acknowledged one NSA officer confidentially. "It will now take us more time to break the new codes, and in the meantime, we will be kept in the dark."

Yet this temporary impediment to comint did nothing to hinder other forms of so-called national technical means of espionage that would prove just as valuable to the mounting U.S. campaign against Qadafi. In responding to the La Belle bombing, the United States would rely heavily on sophisticated electronic sensors—stationed on land or aboard ships, airborne in planes, built into satellites orbiting earth—able to listen in on the blizzard of electromagnetic pulses emanating from Libya's air-defense radars and to take pictures of not only Qadafi's entire military establishment but even the dictator's own quarters.

Since the murders at the Rome airport—and in anticipation of an order to hammer Libya sooner or later—the Air Force in recent months had stepped up its program of photographic intelligence, or photint, aimed at mapping targets for potential U.S. air strikes against Libya and pinpointing the location of Libyan radar, anti-aircraft artillery (AAA), and surface-to-air missiles (SAMs) that could endanger such operations should they be ordered. Much of this work was carried out by high-level reconnaissance aircraft such as the redoubtable SR-71 Blackbird. Flying offshore at speeds in excess of mach 3 and at an altitude above 80,000 feet, which placed the plane beyond the reach of Libya's newest SAMs and best interceptors, the SR-71 could photograph the entire coast of Libya to a depth of some forty miles in about thirty minutes.

Imagery from the high-resolution cameras on the Blackbird and other U.S. spyplanes served not only to help intelligence analysts identify targets. Aircrews could use the pictures to study the objective before a raid and to plan the route to the target. Fed into digital computers on board U.S. warplanes, the information would assist the pilots in guiding their aircraft to Tripoli.

Minimizing the risk that planes would be shot down, their crews killed or perhaps captured and put on public display, depended on a special branch of technical espionage—known as electronic intelligence, or elint. In this kind of electronic spying, various planes and Navy vessels collected data on the electromagnetic frequencies and pulse rates of Libyan radars that provided early warning of an attack and locked Libyan SAMs and AAA onto incoming aircraft. Armed with this information, special electronic-warfare (EW) planes accompanying the strike aircraft could transmit confusing signals that would vastly reduce the effectiveness of such systems. Other planes were armed with missiles that could be programmed to home on a radar signal, destroying the source.

For EW aircraft or the antiradar missiles to succeed, however, elint on Libyan radars had to be precise and detailed. Electronic countermeasure pods for jamming enemy radar and the missiles to be fired at them had to be programmed to search for the signals within a fairly narrow frequency range. Lacking this preparation, the systems would have little chance of picking out the signatures of enemy radar from the myriad of transmissions, including friendly radar, that clutter the airwaves.

Of special interest was the radar that guided long-range SA-5s, the most advanced surface-to-air missiles furnished by the Russians to their clients. The SA-5 radar could operate across a wide frequency range of more than 300 megahertz, but every time the Libyans

In the glare of emergency lighting, firemen and police search for clues in the rubble of the La Belle discotheque in West Berlin after a bomb planted in the washroom tore through the building in the early hours of April 5, 1986. Forensic experts later named several individuals as suspects in the bombing of the nightclub, popular among American servicemen and women, but ferreting them out of their sanctuary in East Germany proved impossible.

flicked on the set in response to the approach of an American elint plane, analysts learned more about the specific frequencies to which the Libyans tuned it. On March 24, Navy flights over the Gulf of Sidra had spooked the Libyans into unleashing a pair of SA-5s at jet fighters seventy miles away. Alert E-2C Hawkeye airborne warning and control aircraft picked up the missile launch signal from the radar and warned the American pilots, who combined jamming with swift evasive action to escape. The incident added significantly to the emerging profile of the SA-5 guidance system and furthered the development of countermeasures.

As the bombing of the La Belle discotheque approached, the Pentagon spared no effort to get intelligence on Libya. Even spy satellites—the most precious U.S. reconnaissance assets and normally devoted to surveillance of the Soviet Union—were called into play. Reportedly, some of the clearest views of potential Libyan targets came not from aircraft but from the orbiting KH-11, a satellite that instead of film to take pictures employs computer-age light-sensitive devices like those used by astronomers to capture the faint light emanating from galaxies far away in outer space. From an altitude of nearly 200 miles, the cameras on the KH-11 can resolve objects at the earth's surface in sufficient detail, it is thought, for photo interpreters to judge the type of missile fitted under the wings of interceptors parked on the ground by the contour of its nose.

In addition, a satellite capable of intercepting communications was diverted from its usual orbit over Poland to a path that brought it within range of Libya. Details of the operation remained secret, but such spy satellites have the capacity to pick up long-distance telephone conversations transmitted via microwaves as well as other forms of wireless communications. As one intelligence officer put it, the orbiting U.S. eavesdroppers could record the telephone whispers of a "Soviet commissar in Moscow talking to his mistress in Yalta." No one will say whether the satellite picked up the message that the British overheard in Berlin.

When Reagan gave the Pentagon the go-ahead for an attack, four days after the bombing in Berlin, prospective targets had already been mapped down to the doorstep, Libyan radar effectively sleuthed, and Qadafi's military and diplomatic communications combed to see if the Libyans were expecting an attack.

The Pentagon named the upcoming raid Operation El Dorado Canyon. Five targets were selected for bombing: Qadafi's compound in Tripoli; an air base in Benghazi, 400 miles across the Gulf of Sidra from the capital, and a barracks there that served as the dictator's alternate command post; the military portion of Tripoli's main airfield; and a naval training facility outside the city where terrorists had been schooled in underwater operations.

Qadafi's compound would be the most difficult objective. As one Air Force officer involved in the operation pointed out, the 200-acre enclosure, often occupied by the dictator, members of his family, and his elite security forces, stood "right in the middle of a populated area and in the middle of all their defenses." The goal was not necessarily to kill Qadafi; intelligence reports indicated that he seldom spent two nights in a row at his compound, moving frequently to frustrate any who might have designs on his life. But by striking at his official residence, the United States hoped to impress upon Qadafi the personal risks of sponsoring terrorism.

Pentagon planners assigned the two targets at Benghazi to Navy fighter-bombers from the Sixth Fleet carriers *Coral Sea* and *America*. The attacks on heavily defended Tripoli fell to the Air Force's 48th Tactical Fighter Wing. Based at Lakenheath, England, and equipped with F-111s—smart planes with computerized navigation and attack systems that would let the pilots streak in low, seek out their objectives in the dark, and drop extraordinarily accurate laser-guided bombs (LGBs) on them—the 48th was a natural choice.

The demanding mission was further complicated by the refusal of France and Spain to grant overflight privileges. As a result, the F-111s would have to go via the Strait of Gibraltar to reach Libya, a flight of six and a half hours covering nearly 3,000 miles. Not only would additional aerial refuelings be necessary, but the duration of the trip found the F-111's Achilles heel—a temperamental radar that often malfunctioned on long flights. Moreover, rules of engagement for attacking Qadafi's compound, which were meant to reduce the risk of civilian casualties in the surrounding area, specified that no pilot could release his bombs unless all his aircraft's systems, including the radar, were go. To compensate for inevitably malfunctioning radars and the chance of missing the target even with laser-guided bombs, nine of eighteen F-111s committed to the raid on Tripoli would be sent against Qadafi's compound.

Officers of the 48th TFW had some misgivings about the emphasis that the strike plan placed on that daunting target, but they made the most of their intelligence assets. Working with a detailed aerial photograph of the compound, the wing's chief of offensive operations designated a clearly visible aim point for each of the nine F-111s. The lead plane, for example, would direct its four 2,000-pound LGBs at the air-conditioning unit atop Qadafi's residence.

Once the targets were defined, the pilots used the accumulated photint and elint data to plan an approach to each objective that skirted SAM sites and AAA batteries. The computer then recorded the route selected on a memory cartridge that was plugged into the F-111's computerized navigation system that would help guide the plane within sight of the target.

When the fully laden F-111s took off for Tripoli from Lakenheath at 5:36 p.m. on April 14, they headed south over the Atlantic with their tanker escorts. At about the same time, a Sixth Fleet task force near Sicily, led by the *Coral Sea* and the *America,* picked up speed as evening descended and slipped away from Soviet intelligence-gathering vessels that often shadow the carriers. No one knew whether the Russians would discover the impending attack or whether they would warn Qadafi.

By 1:30 a.m. Tripoli time, the various elements of Operation El Dorado Canyon were bearing down on the Libyan coast. The first stage of the raid capitalized on the painstaking surveillance of Libyan radar locations, techniques, and frequencies. Paving the way were Air Force EF-111A Ravens from Upper Heyford air base, England, and Navy EA-6B Prowlers from the carriers. Both planes are electronic-warfare versions of strike aircraft armed with bombs—crammed with equipment programmed to jam Libyan radar.

Behind the Prowlers came F/A-18 Hornets and A-7E Corsairs armed with antiradar missiles whose guidance systems were keyed to home on the frequencies used by acquisition and fire-control radars that SAMs and AAA relied on. These smart weapons included both Shrikes, which had a range of about ten miles, and the newer high-speed antiradiation missile (HARM), which had a range of thirty miles as well as the ability to continue toward a radar antenna even if the operator turned the set off. HARMs could be launched in the direction of a known radar even before it became active; if the transmitter came on the air, the missile would veer toward it. This capability eliminated the need for the pilot to close in on the radar site and expose himself to a SAM launch before firing.

Altogether, forty-eight Shrikes and HARMS were fired at radars around Tripoli and Benghazi. The missile barrage had the effect of shutting down the Libyan air-defense system, either by destroying radars or by so unnerving the operators of others that they flicked them off. Though the defenders launched many missiles and stitched the sky with AAA, with no radar to direct these efforts, they had little effect. Of the forty-five U.S. attack aircraft involved in the raid, only one went down—an F-111 bomber bound for Qadafi's compound that inexplicably plowed into the sea near Tripoli.

Despite the suppression of Libyan radar, six of the eight remaining F-111s slated to hit Qadafi's sanctuary never did so. The Air Force attributed this disappointing performance (planners had fig-

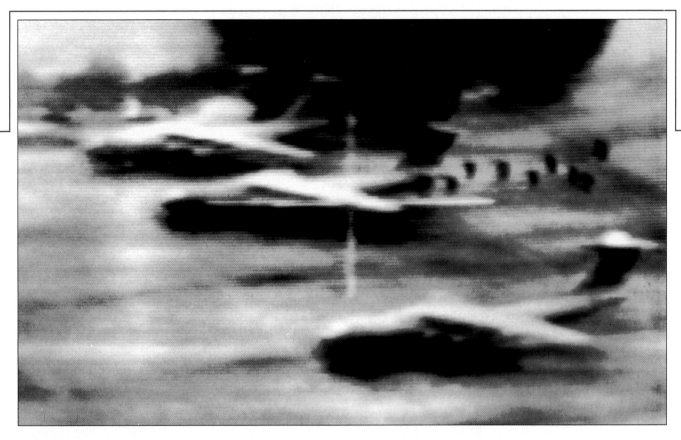

Caught in the infrared imaging system of a U.S. Air Force F-111, Soviet-built Il-76 cargo planes parked on the military ramp of Tripoli airfield are about to be pelted by nine high-drag Mark 82 Snakeyes *(right of cross hairs).* These dumb bombs are slowed by ballutes—helium-filled, mushroom-shaped balloons—on the tail to allow low-flying aircraft to escape their blast. They were used instead of laser-guided bombs against the transports to destroy as many as possible with a single pass.

ured that at least four or five of the nine would make it) to the strain placed on both the planes and their aircrews by the six-hour marathon around Gibraltar. Not only had the men gotten little sleep during the preceding forty-eight hours as they planned the mission, but they flew the entire journey in close formation. The object of this fatiguing tactic was to make four planes appear as one to any radar that might detect them. One pilot became disoriented after refueling and followed the tanker partway home. By the time he realized the error, it was too late to turn around, so he scrubbed. Four others experienced mechanical, electrical, or targeting-system problems and had to cancel their bombing runs in accordance with the strict rules of engagement. The aircrew of the sixth F-111 either misidentified a checkpoint on the coast or the plane's laser-guided bombs malfunctioned, with the result that the ordnance fell on a populous area near the French embassy, killing a number of civilians. The bombs that guided true into the compound succeeded only in destroying the front porch of Qadafi's residence and blowing out windows and doors. Other buildings absorbed similarly moderate damage. However, the point had been made: The Libyan dictator could not feel safe in his own living room.

Better results were had elsewhere. Of the more than 200 bombs dropped on the other four targets by Air Force F-111s and Navy A-6s, only a handful were judged to have missed, causing minor damage in Benghazi. The overall accuracy of the raid was confirmed by U.S.

BENINA AIRFIELD
15 APR 86

DESTROYED F-27

DAMAGED MI-8/HIP

DESTROYED MI-8/HIP

MIG-23/FLOGGER PIECES

DESTROYED MIG-23/FLOGGER

Two poststrike photographs of Benghazi's Benina airfield taken by an Air Force SR-71 Blackbird the day after the raid show the destruction or damage of three Mi-8 helicopters, an F-27 transport plane, and at least three MiG-23 Flogger interceptors. Flying at more than 2,000 miles per hour, the high-altitude reconnaissance SR-71 automatically moves the film to compensate for its speed and produce such sharp images.

spyplanes, including SR-71 Blackbirds that entered Libyan air space to assess the damage. Their photographs, taken from an altitude of about fifteen miles, allowed intelligence officers to examine the debris of MiG-23s on the Benghazi airstrip as if viewing the scene from a helicopter a few hundred feet above the tarmac.

As the Libyan government claimed, probably falsely, that Qadafi's adopted daughter had been killed and other members of his family wounded during the attack on the compound, U.S. eavesdroppers monitored various lines of communication within Libya for word of Qadafi. For two days, there was none. Then on April 16, he appeared briefly on Libyan television. He charged President Reagan with murder for bombing civilians and pledged to continue pressing for "revolution everywhere in the world." The dictator seemed distracted, and the tone of his voice was uncommonly subdued, but he had survived.

Intelligence analysts would long debate the Libya raid and the events that led up to it. Some questioned the haste with which the Reagan administration had pounced on the April 4 Berlin intercepts to make policy without first having them evaluated by NSA experts. One agency official later complained that sending raw data of that kind to the White House "constitutes misuse, because there's nobody there who's capable of interpreting it." Perhaps so, but no evidence has surfaced that the cables from Berlin to Tripoli referred to anything other than the La Belle bombing. Even news reports the following May of possible Syrian complicity in the incident cannot challenge the fact of Libyan involvement. And Reagan singled out Qadafi not because he was the sole sponsor of international terrorism but because he was the most vocal—and the most vulnerable.

The lingering questions concerning the clash with Libya underscored the difficulty of lifting the veil of secrecy cloaking high-stakes intelligence operations. In such cases, even experts privy to classified documents sometimes have found it hard to separate the nuggets of genuine information from the fool's gold, and the best efforts of others to sift through the available evidence and discover the truth inevitably leave gaps in the story. But if certain aspects of El Dorado Canyon remained obscure, one thing was clear: Without electronic spying, the operation would not have been possible. Comint had provided the justification, photint had pinned down the targets, and elint had reduced the risks to an acceptable level.

These three shadowy branches of intelligence gathering, rooted in the first half of the twentieth century, grew explosively during the Cold War. Photographic systems have moved beyond Kodak film exposed in cameras carried by low-flying aircraft to electronic sensors mounted in the focal planes of huge telescopes aimed at earth from orbiting satellites. New radar systems yield startling detail in images taken at night or through cloud cover now made as transparent as glass. In a comparable upsurge of technology, the capabilities of equipment used to gather electronic and communications intelligence have been vastly expanded. Not only has such gear also found its way into space, but it has been linked to ranks of high-speed computers that make it possible to sift rapidly through vast quantities of data to find the significant clue. As the events surrounding the bombing of the La Belle discotheque show, such capacities have become a vital means of unmasking enemies, laying bare their designs, and acting against them.　★

As seen in this head-on view, the SR-71's engines angled down and in, aligning them with the flow of air from the nose to improve thrust. Two vertical stabilizers, or tails, mounted on the engine nacelles doubled as rudders, turning in their entirety to keep the plane from spinning if an engine had an "unstart" *(page 28)*. The size of a small airliner, the Blackbird was the first stealth aircraft. Its stabilizers, canted fifteen degrees, and its chines—tapered horizontal surfaces along the fuselage for increased lift—cut radar reflections, making the SR-71 difficult to detect.

Spyplane
Supreme

A superplane, its handlers called it. Powered by two monster engines set in a delta-shaped blade of wing, the SR-71 Blackbird was speed incarnate, a manned bullet that skimmed across the top of the atmosphere at better than 2,000 miles per hour. Fewer than three dozen were built, and only a few hundred pilots and reconnaissance systems officers (RSOs) ever entered its two-seat cockpit and, outrunning the sound of their own engines, rode in silence as the world slid by more than 80,000 feet below. But for twenty-four years, from 1966 until 1990, the SR-71 reaped a priceless harvest of intelligence with its keen-eyed cameras, cloud-piercing radar, and electronic-intercept instruments. So high and fast did it fly that not a single Blackbird was shot down, despite perhaps a thousand attempts.

The SR-71 demanded technological pioneering. Kelly Johnson, who oversaw its creation at the Lockheed Skunk Works—nickname for the company's Advanced Development Projects Unit—in the early 1960s, observed almost in wonderment, "I think I can truly say that everything on the aircraft—from rivets and fluids, up through materials and power plants—had to be invented from scratch."

To withstand the searing temperatures of mach 3-plus flight, the plane was fashioned mostly of titanium and given several specialized defenses against heat, from tires filled with the inert gas nitrogen for reducing the fire hazard in case of a blowout in flight to control cables made of a high-strength alloy used in watch springs. Gold plating on fuel and oil lines reflected heat to help keep them cool. The huge engines, housed in nacelles with a diameter greater than that of the fuselage, were built for continuous afterburning, unique among jet power plants.

Although the SR-71 would finally be retired largely for budgetary reasons, its performance limits—somewhere beyond mach 4 and an altitude of 100,000 feet—are likely to remain unmatched for years to come.

A Racing Engine
Built for the Heights

"The SR-71," said one of its pilots, "is only designed to do a few things—like going very high and going very fast." For both, the starting point was power, vast amounts of it. The source was a pair of Pratt & Whitney J-58 engines, each generating 32,500 pounds of thrust, equivalent to the output of forty-five diesel locomotives.

Used in no other plane, the engine was an innovative blend of two approaches to jet propulsion. At lower altitudes and speeds, the J-58 functioned as a conventional turbojet: Air entering the engine was compressed by turbine blades for efficient combustion when fuel was mixed in. At high altitudes and speeds, the job of air compression was accomplished mostly by the ramming effect of the plane's forward motion: As the Blackbird hurtled ahead, each J-58 swallowed an immense volume of air. In effect, the inlet became a supercharger, accounting for 60 percent of total thrust at cruise speed. The afterburner provided 30 percent, the remainder coming from the conventional turbojet portion of the J-58.

The key to the ramming effect was a large cone, or spike, that automatically extended or retracted as much as twenty-six inches to direct the shock wave formed at supersonic speeds into the inlet, greatly increasing airflow. Vigorous maneuvering or a sudden change in air temperature could alter the shape of the shock wave faster than the spike could adjust to the changing conditions, popping the shock wave out of the nacelle. Called an "unstart," this event caused a dramatic loss of thrust on one side of the plane that jolted it violently, sometimes enough to bash the pilot's helmeted head against the canopy. Instantly, automatic controls angled the aircraft's vertical stabilizers to keep it flying straight, while simultaneously unstarting the other engine to equalize thrust. Within a few seconds, both spikes adjusted themselves to the proper position, ending the episode.

A movable cone set in the inlet of the J-58 was the primary means of governing airflow into the engine; it began to retract at a speed of mach 1.6 and altitude of about 35,000 feet. Several valves, vanes, and doors fine-tuned the flow. Because of high operating temperatures, the engine required a special oil, almost solid below thirty degrees Fahrenheit. As hydraulic fluid for engine control devices, the SR-71 used its own fuel, circulating it through hydraulic actuators before injecting it into the combustion chambers.

A Design for Scorching Speed

As a Blackbird sliced through the thin reaches of the upper atmosphere at thirty-five miles per minute, friction heated leading edges to an average of 550 degrees Fahrenheit—and as much as 1,200 degrees Fahrenheit at some points around the engines. No ordinary aircraft could withstand such searing temperatures, but the SR-71 was at home in its self-made inferno. Its black finish—glowing indigo blue at the cruise speed of mach 3.2—helped cool the plane by radiating three times as much heat as bare metal would. Fully 93 percent of the plane was made of titanium, which offered great strength and heat resistance while weighing half as much as stainless steel, the only other metal capable of enduring the Blackbird's operating conditions.

Even the fuel had to be heat resistant. The SR-71 ran on a special hydrocarbon diet called JP-7, with a high flash point that minimized the chances of a spontaneous explosion as heat spread through the airframe. To ignite this recalcitrant fuel required the use of a highly unstable chemical called triethyl borane. A small amount injected into the engine's combustion chambers or afterburner exploded on contact with air, producing enough heat to set the JP-7 aflame.

In effect, the SR-71 was a flying fuel tank: JP-7 filled two-thirds of the fuselage and half the wing. But it was not held in ordinary rubber-lined compartments, since rubber or any other leakproof lining would melt. Instead, the JP-7 was stored directly against the plane's titanium skin. The seams between the titanium panels dribbled fuel profusely at the start of a mission, but as the Blackbird raced to the heights that were its natural realm, the fuel compartments were sealed tight by heat-induced expansion.

To prevent warping of its panels by heat expansion, the wing was grooved longitudinally both top and bottom; as the temperature rose, the corrugations deepened without disrupting the airflow. After each flight, five airframe specialists spent six hours inspecting the plane for heat damage. Anything containing chlorine, which eats titanium, was kept away. So corrosive to the metal is chlorine that distilled water was used to wash parts during manufacture; small amounts of the chemical in municipal water supplies could have caused cracks.

Survival Tactics for a Rarefied Domain

Flying fifteen miles above the earth, the pilot and RSO of an SR-71 were enveloped by dangers—oven-hot surfaces (the canopy's Plexiglas reached temperatures in excess of 600 degrees Fahrenheit), and an outer environment where the air was seventy-five degrees below zero and so low in pressure that it would cause blood to boil. But the crewmen were well cocooned against these threats. The cabin was air-conditioned to a comfortable sixty degrees, and it was also pressurized like the cabin of an airliner. Nonetheless, the crew wore pressure suits in case they had to abandon the aircraft. The suits were sturdy enough to permit safe ejection from the plane at mach 4 and an altitude of more than 100,000 feet. Indeed, crews ejected from Blackbirds in situations ranging from sitting still on the ground to traveling at mach 3 and 80,000 feet. All survived.

A reconnaissance run in an SR-71 was demanding at the best of times. Traveling at three times the speed of sound, the plane had to remain rock-steady and hold exactly on its intended course. "If you are a mile off in six hours on a reconnaissance mission," said one pilot, "you might as well have stayed in bed." Blackbirds used an extremely accurate astronavigation system (ANS) that took continual fixes on three stars selected from a star catalog for the SR-71's flight track that was loaded into the navigational computer hours before the mission. The ANS also supplied position updates to a backup inertial navigation system. During the surveillance run, a computer did the actual flying while the pilot monitored the plane's performance. Meanwhile, the RSO kept an eye on the various sensors in the Blackbird's nose—high-resolution radar, eavesdropping gear, and cameras that could photograph a thousand square miles in sufficient detail to reveal stripes on a parking lot in good light.

The SR-71's detachable nose, bolted to a bulkhead just ahead of the canopy, carried either an optical camera or a synthetic-aperture radar imaging system *(pages 67-70)*. Other sensors, including elint receivers and a camera that provided a continuous record of the plane's track across the ground, were installed in the chines. The craft's ANS star tracker was mounted on gimbals in a round porthole located between the rear of the canopy and the air-refueling door, outlined in red.

Crossing the World at a Moment's Notice

As it scanned the earth far below, an SR-71 drank its way through a full load of 12,200 gallons of fuel in an hour and a half, covering more than 3,000 miles in the process. Nitrogen was steadily fed into the emptying fuel tanks to keep out any oxygen that could feed a fire. At the same time, pumps shifted the remaining fuel between tanks to keep the plane balanced.

To extend a Blackbird's range, aerial tankers with refills of JP-7 were stationed along its route. Missions often covered immense distances—from Okinawa to Iran and back, for example. Altogether, the peerless spyplanes traversed more than 65 million miles during their nearly quarter-century of service, always unarmed—and also untouchable.

Because of the extreme operating conditions, Blackbirds received forty hours of maintenance on the ground for every hour they spent in the air. But the SR-71 was a sturdy aircraft. None ever needed a wing replacement or even suffered a wing crack. After more than twenty years of service, the planes were actually stronger than when they were built—a result of the annealing of their titanium by the fierce temperatures of flight at more than mach 3.

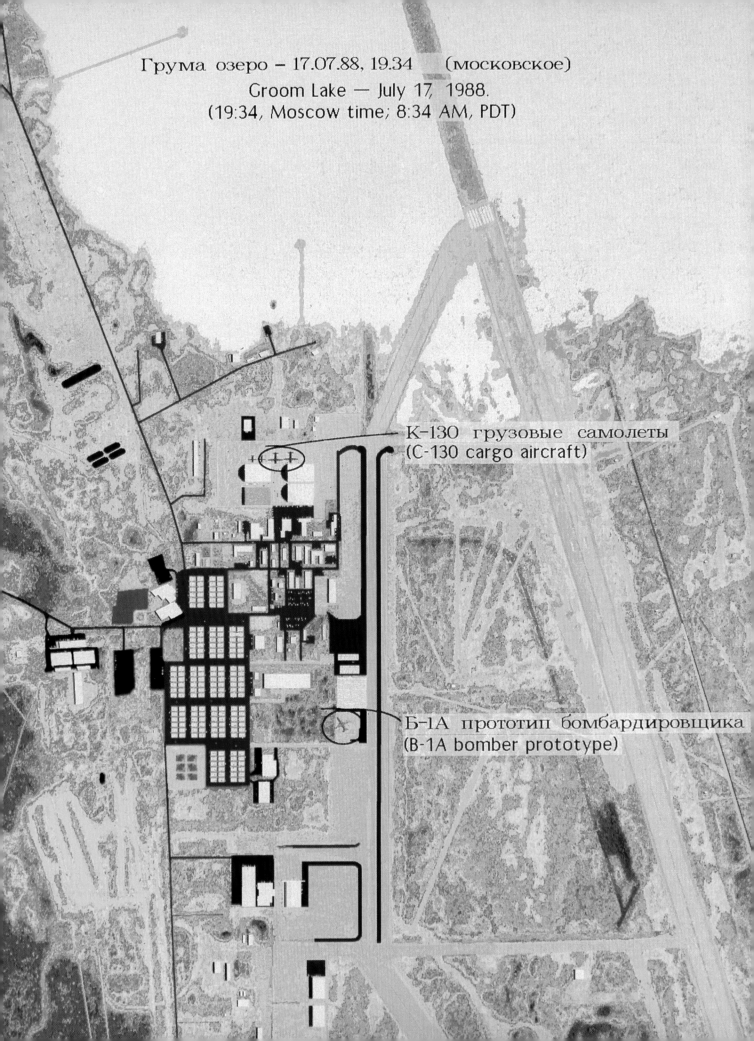

Грума озеро – 17.07.88, 19.34   (московское)
Groom Lake — July 17, 1988.
(19:34, Moscow time; 8:34 AM, PDT)

К-130 грузовые самолеты
(C-130 cargo aircraft)

Б-1А прототип бомбардировщика
(B-1A bomber prototype)

A New Age of Aerial Imagery

Taken by a Soviet satellite flying 170 miles above Nevada, this computer-colored photograph shows Groom Lake airfield, located ninety-five miles northwest of Las Vegas. The secret facility, whose existence the Air Force has never acknowledged, has been used to test not only the B-1 bomber seen here but a variety of other aircraft, including the U-2 and SR-71 spyplanes.

The assignment was routine: Fly from Shaikh Isa air base in Bahrain to southern Iraq and take pictures of five Iraqi airfields. Two RF-4Cs, reconnaissance versions of the Vietnam-era Phantom fighter-bomber, would take off, refuel on the way to the target, cruise over the airfields at an altitude of 20,000 feet and a speed of about 500 knots for the photo run, then turn homeward with the take. Upon landing, technicians would pull film cartridges from the lead aircraft—the second served as a backup—and develop their contents. Within minutes, the pilot and weapons system officer (WSO), who sat in the backseat of the F-4 and doubled as navigator and sensor operator, would be pointing out details on the film as photo interpreters unreeled it across a light table.

As Operation Desert Storm got under way in January 1991, dozens of such flights were dispatched daily. The goal of each was to return with evidence of destruction wrought by earlier air strikes against Iraq's army and air force or to document new targets worthy of attention by the international coalition of air forces assembled to help drive Iraq from Kuwait, seized the preceding summer on orders from Iraqi dictator Saddam Hussein.

Captain John Grevin was the WSO in the backup Phantom assigned to the mission. Both of the aircraft and their crews had arrived from Bergstrom Air Force Base, Texas, with the rest of the 12th Tactical Reconnaissance Squadron on January 14, just weeks earlier. Already Grevin and the pilot, Captain Pat O'Brien, had flown some eighteen sorties, each little more eventful than the preceding one. Today's would be different.

They were "about fifteen miles south of Jalībah," Grevin later recalled, "when we started getting a lot of indication in the cockpit that we were being tracked by an SA-6 battery." These Soviet-built surface-to-air missiles, whose radar had triggered a warning system

37

aboard the plane, have an effective ceiling of approximately 60,000 feet, quite high enough to pose a serious threat to the two Phantoms. "I looked over my right shoulder," said Grevin, "and saw a missile come up through the clouds. I called a break-turn for the flight, and Pat broke right. The lead aircraft didn't hear the call but saw us turn and started to turn for himself. He saw the missile pass about 1,500 feet behind our tail."

Resuming course toward the target, the two planes again began to receive missile warnings, and Grevin saw a second SA-6. "This time," he said, "we jettisoned our external stores, punched off chaff, flares, and used ECM and finally defeated the missile." Maneuvering the aircraft to avoid the SAMs had burned precious fuel, and without external tanks, the planes had an insufficient reserve to reach their objective and return home, so O'Brien turned south and headed back to Shaikh Isa.

Captains O'Brien and Grevin—and other aviators like them—share a professional family tree that can be traced back to 1794 when French Revolutionary Army observers reconnoitered the town of Maubeuge from wicker gondolas slung under tethered hot-air balloons. The first military use of the airplane during World War I was for observation. In those early days, the pilot had to rely solely on his memory to report what he had seen on the other side of no man's land, but soon cameras became airborne, and the field of photographic intelligence—photint—was born. Technology advanced rapidly to the point that a picture taken from a height of 15,000 feet could be magnified to show an infantryman's footprints. By 1918, aerial reconnaissance had proved so useful to all of the combatants that they employed almost 90,000 people to produce more than 12,000 photographic prints a day. The importance of spying by air even prompted the development of a new breed of aircraft, the fighter, whose primary mission was to shoot down the scout planes before they could return to base with their precious information.

And thus began a contest that continues unabated today, with the observer seeking protection in greater speed, higher altitude, or a combination of the two—while the quarry strives to bring him down by means of ever more capable arrows. In World War II, virtually every high-flying bomber or fast fighter had a version that was modified for reconnaissance missions. Twin-boomed American P-38 Lightning fighters and nimble British de Havilland Mosquito fighter-bombers were fitted with special nose cameras so that they might dart over enemy territory and outrace the interceptors sent up to shoot them down. And with the development of the German Me-262, the first photoreconnaissance jets were born. In Korea, jets came into their own. Specially adapted RF-80s and RB-45s braved "MiG Alley" continuously to photograph enemy positions, airfields, troop movements, and supply routes for rapid inclusion in target lists.

Most of these photint efforts bent toward gathering tactical intelligence, the kind of information that might assist a commander in planning the next day's action. But with the Cold War had come a greater need than ever for a different kind of fact—strategic intelligence that might shed light on the Soviet Union's ability to prevail in a third conflict of global scale. The United States, both as the guardian of its own security and as the leader of NATO, and the Soviet Union sought such information, but America took the lead in aerial reconnaissance—and would keep it through the end of the military competition with the Soviets.

Inasmuch as the aircraft used for tactical recce had neither the range for nor the ability to survive a peek deep inside the USSR, new planes took to the skies. The first could fly 4,000 miles unrefueled and rise so high that it could not be shot down. As Soviet air defenses improved and altitude failed as a shield, a new plane appeared that was endowed with blinding speed and the ability to pass close to enemy radar without being detected. Meanwhile, satellites circled earth hundreds of miles up in space while traveling at thousands of miles per hour carrying remarkable new sensors that brought photint into the electronic age.

As the vantage point moved ever farther from the surface of the planet, however, the difficulties of acquiring clear images of objects on the ground increased much faster than the height of the vantage point. To overcome them, optical scientists and engineers had to design better lenses. Chemists had to concoct improved photographic films that combined short exposure time with the ability to record fine detail. Light-sensitive computer chips would supplant film in some applications, slashing the time between the instant of exposure and the arrival of an image at a photo interpreter's work station. Consisting of the ones-and-zeros language that computers understand, such images also permitted these powerful electronic number-crunchers to clarify the picture by eliminating atmospheric dust and smoke that, even on a cloudless day, can obscure details on the ground. Computers also help analysts probe the images in new ways. Moreover, a remarkable kind of radar—capable of producing images of near-photographic quality, day or night, clear skies or cloudy—came of age.

Cameras Instead of Guns

In early 1961, the remote, landlocked country of Laos in southeast Asia was mired in a smoldering civil war. The Royal Laotian government requested help from the U.S. Air Force in locating concentrations of Communist Pathet Lao guerrillas. In response, a detachment from the 45th Tactical Reconnaissance Squadron (TRS) arrived at Don Muang airfield, Thailand. Equipped with RF-101C Voodoos—unarmed, modified copies of the twin-engine, supersonic F-101B fighter—the 45th flew sorties over both Laos and South Vietnam, where American advisers were helping the government in its own civil war against Communist insurgents. By 1964, American participation in the defense of the Saigon government had escalated to the point that U.S. Air Force F-100 fighter-bombers had been committed to the effort. Voodoos accompanied the planes to their targets, lingering briefly to photograph bomb damage before returning to base. Soon, there was more action than one squadron could handle. So in April 1965, another detachment from the 45th TRS and one from the 20th TRS deployed to Southeast Asia, setting up shop in Udorn, Thailand, to cover Laos.

Soon, the Voodoos in Thailand also began flying missions over North Vietnam, and it was there that the recon pilots faced unprecedented danger. By mid-1966, North Vietnamese air defenses boasted a vast array of the most modern equipment their Soviet and Chinese allies could supply. In June alone, seven RF-101s were lost. Some pilots began to doubt whether they could live up to their motto: Alone, Unarmed, and Unafraid. Flying north was beginning to give them the jitters.

Early on May 21, 1967, two RF-101s of the 20th TRS took off from Udorn to photograph the Bac Mai motor pool at the southern edge of Hanoi. Led by Lieutenant Colonel Paul Nelson, the aircraft sped toward the bristling defenses of the enemy capital. Radar-guided

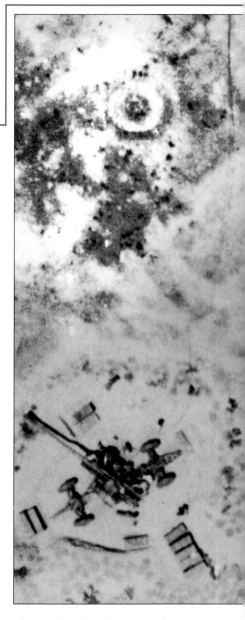

Flying at low altitude to avoid detection, an unarmed RF-101 Voodoo, principal reconnaissance jet during the early years of the Vietnam War, captures its own shadow as it passes over a North Vietnamese 57-mm antiaircraft site in 1966. Two guns with boxes of ammunition stacked nearby can be seen in the picture, one in the lower left corner and another near the plane's shadow in the upper right corner.

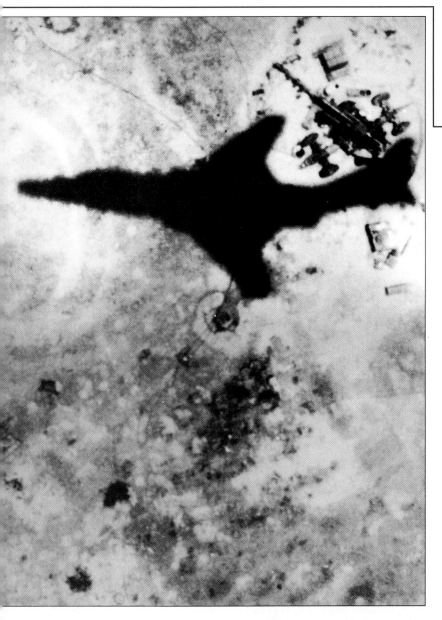

SA-2 missiles and antiaircraft artillery (AAA) batteries, ranging in size from 23 to 85 millimeters, ringed the city, covering all approaches. Nearing their goal, the Voodoos turned onto their final heading, screaming just above the deck at 540 knots. When they were almost on top of the target, Nelson and his wingman pulled back on their sticks and slammed their throttles forward into afterburner as they climbed to 12,000 feet or so for the photo run.

Both ships ran the gauntlet unscathed, with nothing but their pilots' skills to help them dodge the SAMs and evade all of the AAA fire as well. After getting their pictures, they headed for home. As they began their final approach to land at Udorn, Lieutenant Colonel James Brickel, commander of the 20th, and his wingman were rolling into position for takeoff on another mission through the Hanoi area. Brickel keyed his microphone when he sighted the returning airplanes and asked for a report. Nelson, still agitated forty-five minutes after his chain of close calls south of Hanoi, radioed that more than twenty SAMs had been fired at them.

Brickel gritted his teeth and advanced his throttles. He and his wingman flew north until they crossed the Red River approximately seventy-five miles northwest of Hanoi. Hugging the deck as Nelson had done, the pair dashed toward the North Vietnamese capital, afterburners lit.

"Our target was the Kinh No motor pool, which was just north of the city," Brickel later recounted. "But before we got there, twenty to twenty-five SA-2s were fired at us. To evade them, my wingman and I began to scissor, flying back and forth over each other, to confuse the radar operators that guided them." At one point, two missiles sliced between the planes, two went behind Brickel, and two more streaked over him and disappeared in the sky above. "We turned our cameras on as we approached the target and just let them run. As soon as we got our film, we turned out to the Gulf of Tonkin to link up with a refueling tanker. By the time we returned to Udorn, between the two flights, forty-five to fifty missiles had been fired. There were only something like three ready missiles left in all of North Vietnam when the strike flight arrived about fifteen minutes later."

Despite their poor marksmanship on that day, on others the North Vietnamese succeeded in downing U.S. reconnaissance jets, more of them by AAA than with SAMs. They also sent their small but potent fleet of MiGs against the planes. In September 1967, after

a MiG-21 managed to shoot down an RF-101, all Voodoos in the theater were redeployed to Tan Son Nhut Airbase at Saigon and restricted to operations over Laos and South Vietnam. The U.S. Air Force also changed its defensive tactics, abandoning the "Lone Ranger" approach of Nelson and Brickel and assigning recon missions an escort of up to four fighters, known as MiGCAP.

Replacing the Voodoo over the North and in Laos along the Ho Chi Minh Trail was the RF-4C, a derivative of the workhorse mach 2 Phantom II fighter. Its elongated nose contained a large bay that could house a variety of sensors and cameras, depending on the mission. Framing cameras, which take a series of partially overlapping photos with either 4.5-by-4.5-inch or 9-by-9-inch negatives, could be mounted to shoot obliquely ahead of the plane or to either side. Panoramic cameras, using a rotating prism, could take a picture below the aircraft stretching from horizon to horizon. At night, when the Voodoo had been blind, photoflash cartridges shot from ejector racks in the fuselage near the tail enabled RF-4Cs to take pictures after dark with standard film. An infrared imaging system and film, also for use at night, could record the presence of trucks or aircraft, for example, based on differences in temperature.

Major Larry Krull piloted an RF-4C out of Udorn with the 14th Tactical Reconnaissance Squadron. "We had a thing we ran at first light in the morning called the 'truck line,'" he remembered. "We would run up and down all the routes in Laos along the Ho Chi Minh Trail where the guys flying at night in the gunships had claimed they had shot up trucks, but the next day there would be no evidence of anything knocked out. It was pretty discouraging until they called us in and we started flying with them at night using our infrared cameras. We were then able to pick up those targets that had been struck before they could be bulldozed off the trail. Now we knew that our strikes were working. It was a great boost in morale to the gunship guys."

Taking pictures and getting the film safely back to base was only the tip of the photoreconnaissance iceberg. As soon as a recce bird rolled to a stop, teams of technicians swarmed over the airplane. They dropped the

Lieutenant Colonel James Brickel leans against the wing of his RF-101 Voodoo, pierced by a large chunk of shrapnel from an 85-mm AAA round that exploded below the aircraft on one of the pilot's many flights over North Vietnam. Hit as he approached the target, a steel mill, Brickel managed to get his pictures and return safely to Thailand even though the shell, he said later, "blew the engine bay door off, hit the left aileron, and filled the cockpit with smoke."

43

camera bay door in the nose and pulled the film magazines for processing, just as they would nearly twenty years later in Bahrain. These were rushed to an air-conditioned building or van where they were processed into negatives for photo interpreters (PIs) to analyze. Taking every possible precaution to protect the imagery from fingerprints and contamination by dust, the PIs quickly examined the negatives on light tables. By comparing the images to maps, they could rapidly determine whether the crew had found and photographed the correct target.

After a postflight inspection of their airplane, the pilot and his backseater spoke to the PI. For five to ten minutes they described not only what they had photographed but what they had seen with the "Mark I Human Eyeball." After they left, the PIs went over the images again, looking for fleeting targets such as troops or trucks on the move. If any were found—and attack aircraft available—a strike package was immediately dispatched. Then followed a more detailed study of the photographs. Staff Sergeant Steven Pagel, a PI with the 432d Reconnaissance Technical Squadron at Udorn, explained this step: "In phase two, we had more time to study the imagery. Using stereoscopes—two magnifying eyepieces on wire legs—and light tables, we could overlap the negatives for a three-dimensional effect. This really made things stand out. We could note new techniques in enemy camouflage, bomb damage, and other things not apparent at first look. If we saw something really good we got on the phone to squadron headquarters immediately. The system worked pretty good, but it was still 'stubby pencil' work compared to the systems that came later."

To the Edge of Space

Long before the United States became enmeshed in Vietnam, it had joined a battle of wits and intimidation with the Soviet Union, in which each nation, so suspicious and fearful of the other's warlike capabilities and intentions, took the most extraordinary measures to find out what the other side was up to. Though planes could peer across the borders of some of the USSR's East European satellites—and into a few places in the Soviet Union itself—the Russian heartland was inaccessible to overhead photography. Not only were there no aircraft that could make the trip or survive it in the face of

In a rare sequence taken over Hanoi in 1967 by the panoramic camera in the lead aircraft of a two-ship flight of RF-4C recon planes, a North Vietnamese SA-2 missile shoots down the leader's wingman. The missile can be seen at the bottom of the frame at far left approaching the U.S. jet at the top of the picture. Seconds later *(left)*, the warhead explodes, setting the plane on fire. Both crewmen ejected but were soon captured; the pilot later died in captivity.

the inevitable opposition, but flying without permission over another nation's territory violated international law.

In 1954, a committee of reconnaissance specialists from the CIA and the Air Force met. Chaired by Richard Bissell, special assistant to CIA Director Allen Dulles, the group secretly commissioned an aircraft to fill the important strategic role of spying on the number of Soviet strategic bombers and ballistic missiles, thought to be growing at a dangerous rate. Designated the U-2—a *nom de guerre,* since the U stood for utility—the plane was intended to solve the problems of range and vulnerability linked to other reconnaissance planes while simply ignoring the legal issue. Unless the Soviets could catch such an airplane in the act of violating their sovereignty, any complaint would merely pit their charges against America's denials. The contract signed between Bissell's committee and Lockheed Aircraft Corporation called for an airplane that could provide a stable camera platform while flying above 70,000 feet, well beyond the capabilities of any interceptor, rocket, or missile of the day. It was also to have an operational range greater than 4,000 miles.

Lockheed's premier designer, Clarence L. "Kelly" Johnson, and a handpicked team from the Advanced Development Projects Unit had studied the strict—and unprecedented—specifications even before the contract was awarded. Johnson was the perfect choice to head the project. He had been instrumental in the unique design of the P-38 Lightning fighter of World War II; the triple-tailed Constellation airliner; the P-80 Shooting Star, America's first operational jet fighter; and the F-104 Starfighter, a mach 2 interceptor and fighter-bomber—and the fastest jet of its day. All were innovative ventures, demonstrations of Johnson's belief that any challenge could be met with inspired engineering.

Johnson's team, laboring in a facility dubbed the Skunk Works

45

after a cave where secret formulas were concocted in Al Capp's "Li'l Abner" cartoon strip, initially offered a quick and easy solution—or so it appeared. They proposed a relatively simple modification of the stubby-winged F-104, grafted with longer wings to provide lift in the thin air at 70,000 feet. But the F-104 fuselage could not accommodate the only existing power plant capable of operating at such high altitudes—the Pratt & Whitney J-57 jet engine. Designing a new engine specifically for the modified F-104 would be time-consuming and inordinately expensive. Johnson admitted later, "it soon became obvious that the only equipment we might retain from the F-104 might be the rudder pedals."

The Skunk Works design team judged that, to perform well more than thirteen miles above sea level, the U-2 should resemble a sailplane. Final plans called for long, straight wings (they would have a span of seventy-nine feet, as large as those of the Convair 340, a fifty-passenger airliner of that time), along with oversize tail and control surfaces. Starting from scratch also enabled the team to incorporate the J-57 engine.

In December 1954, Lockheed began building the prototype at its Palmdale, California, plant. On July 29, 1955, the first U-2, nick-named Kelly's Angel, took to the air—much to the consternation of its pilot. "It was supposed to be a taxi test with Tony LeVier at the controls," related Johnson. "The airplane was so light that on his second taxi run, it just lifted to a height of about thirty-five feet. And when he tried to land, the darned airplane didn't want to. It could fly at idle power on the engine. He managed to bounce it down, and in the process bent the tail gear a bit. But we soon had it fixed."

Six days later, the aircraft was first flown intentionally from a secret test site at Groom Lake, Nevada. With LeVier again at the controls, the U-2 climbed effortlessly to 8,000 feet. "The airplane flew beautifully," said Kelly Johnson, who had observed the flight from a C-47 chase plane, "but again Tony had trouble on landing. We discovered the airplane makes a fine landing when the tail wheel hits at the same time or slightly ahead of the main gear." Like other aspects of the U-2, its undercarriage resembled that of a sail-plane, with a single wheel—the main gear—positioned under the fuselage near the leading edge of the wings and a smaller tail wheel farther back. The long, sagging wings were supported by tiny out-rigger wheels that fell away as the wings straightened during the takeoff run. Metal endplates on the wing tips prevented damage during landings as the wings drooped to touch the runway.

Four days after the aircraft's maiden flight, Lockheed invited CIA and Air Force representatives to witness the first official test. This time, Kelly's Angel climbed to 35,000 feet in less than five minutes and could have easily gone much higher. The government delegation was impressed. "From then on it was drive, drive, drive," recalled Johnson. "Build the airplanes, get them in operation, train ground and flight crews, maintenance men, military pilots." It was a giddy time for the Skunk Works. Eight months later, the U-2s became operational.

The initial contingent of pilots were Air Force officers loaned to the CIA and trained to fly the U-2 at Groom Lake. Before long, however, the CIA began to hire former U.S. Air Force pilots to fly the high-altitude spyplane. The first U-2 unit deployed to Lakenheath airfield in England in April 1956, bearing the Air Force cover name First Weather Reconnaissance Squadron (Provisional). Additional aircraft were deployed, not coincidentally, to countries bordering the Soviet Union. In all, three Weather Reconnaissance Squadrons were formed. The Second WRS(P) was deployed to Incirlik Airfield, Turkey, and the Third WRS(P) to Atsugi, Japan. Each WRS(P) had "operating locations"—Wiesbaden and Giebelstadt in West Germany, Bodo in Norway, and Peshawar and Lahore in Pakistan, for example—to serve as start or end points for flights across different areas of the USSR.

Mounted in the bellies of the U-2s were specially designed Hycon Model 73B cameras, large-format instruments that produced negatives measuring nine by eighteen inches. Using a lens having a focal length of three feet and highly sensitive, fine-grain film developed by Kodak, this remarkable camera could take photos from 70,000 feet that could discern a two-inch object. Despite its capabilities, the Model 73B could not penetrate the obscuring effects of haze and dust that often pervade the atmosphere. Thus U-2 missions were often scheduled to follow the passage of a cold front through the target area to take advantage of the crystal-clear air that usually trails this meteorological event.

In July of 1955, as the first U-2s approached operational status, President Dwight Eisenhower offered the Soviet Union a plan called Open Skies. It entailed an exchange of information on strategic weapon sites and free access by aerial reconnaissance to inspect those facilities. At that time, the Soviets would have none of it, labeling the Open Skies proposal "nothing more than a bald espionage plot."

Spy missions began without the agreement in 1956. The long excursions were explained to the press as "high-altitude meteorological research flights." One such cruise was credited with providing 4,000 pictures of a swath of Soviet territory between twenty-five and thirty miles wide over a distance of 2,160 miles. An autopilot assisted the pilot during such a mission in holding the U-2 at a constant altitude. Variations in speed also had to be avoided. At 70,000 feet, there was only a ten-knot margin between stalling speed, below which the airplane would be moving too slowly to fly, and mach 1, where the fragile aircraft would shake itself to pieces.

For nearly four years, the U-2s overflew the Soviet Union without mishap. They brought back precious photographs of Soviet strategic installations, confirming that the USSR was, if anything, behind the United States in intercontinental ballistic missiles (ICBMs) and long-range bombers. Though the Kremlin quietly gnashed its teeth, nothing was said publicly—by either side. The Soviets made numerous attempts to shoot down the elusive high fliers without success. U-2 pilots watched in fascination as MiG-19 fighters tried vainly to intercept, but they could not come close; maximum altitude for the MiG-19 and even for the more advanced MiG-21 was a mere 50,000 feet. The MiG-21, however, could approach several thousand feet nearer by accelerating to top speed and zooming upward, but it inevitably stalled in the thin air, lost control, and tumbled back into the lower atmosphere before coming within missile range. The Soviets' first SAM, the SA-1, could do no better. Upon seeing U-2 photos

A prisoner of the Cold War, U-2
pilot Francis Gary Powers wears
the prison clothes his Russian
captors provided him. The Russians displayed this photo and
the wreckage of Powers's plane
to prove that President Eisenhower had lied about U-2 flights
over the Soviet Union. Powers
was released in February 1962,
exchanged for a Soviet spy.

with as many as thirty-five MiGs obscuring the view of the ground, Kelly Johnson coined a name for the air show: the aluminum cloud.

But on May 1, 1960, the situation changed abruptly and dramatically. CIA pilot Francis Gary Powers, flying a U-2 on a mission from Peshawar, Pakistan, to Bodo, Norway, had just passed over the city of Sverdlovsk, 900 miles east of Moscow, when an orange light filled his cockpit and he heard a dull thump. The cause remains unknown, but it is probable that one of a barrage of new Soviet SA-2 surface-to-air missiles had exploded near him. Powers fought a losing battle to maintain control of his damaged aircraft. "A violent movement shook the plane," Powers wrote later, "flinging me all over the cockpit. I assumed both wings had come off. What was left of the plane began spinning, the nose pointed upward toward the sky. All I could see was the sky, spinning, spinning." Eschewing his ejection seat, which most U-2 pilots incorrectly believed to have been rigged by the CIA to explode when activated, Powers managed to open his canopy manually and jump from the cockpit. He was captured almost immediately upon landing, and within four days, his story could be read in newspapers around the world.

The shootdown was extremely embarrassing to President Eisenhower, who, believing that Powers died in the crash, had initially denied that the incident involved a U.S. spyplane on a deliberate overflight of the USSR. Soviet Premier Nikita Khrushchev played the incident for all that it was worth, parading the captured American airman before the cameras, canceling an upcoming summit meeting with Eisenhower, and displaying the wreckage of the U-2 in Moscow's Gorki Park. Powers was convicted of espionage and sentenced to ten years in prison. A chastened American administration immediately ceased the overflights and promised that they would not resume.

Two years later, the U-2s found another venue for their activities, this time much closer to home. During the spring and summer of 1962, U.S. intelligence sources reported an increase in ship traffic between the Soviet Union and Cuba. On August 29, a CIA U-2 operating out of Florida brought back film of Cuba showing two Soviet SA-2 missile sites completed and several more under construction. Of itself, this was not cause for undue alarm; SAMs are

49

a short-range, defensive weapon posing no threat to the continental United States. But Colonel John Wright, an intelligence expert who analyzed the film, was disturbed by the trapezoidal, four-launcher configuration of the SAM sites. In earlier U-2 photos taken over the Soviet Union, he had seen that pattern used only in air-defense networks surrounding nuclear-missile installations. Elsewhere, the launchers formed a hexagon.

When informed of the SAM developments in Cuba, President John F. Kennedy, Eisenhower's successor, immediately ordered an increase in surveillance flights by U-2s. In September, reports from Cubans fleeing their Communist homeland indicated that two Soviet freighters had delivered a shipment of rockets, possibly SS-4 medium-range ballistic missiles capable of striking cities in the United States southeast of an arc stretching from Washington, D.C., to San Antonio, Texas.

Even though no physical or visual evidence of SS-4s could be found, tension rose in Washington, creating an almost warlike atmosphere. The U-2 sortie rate was stepped up to one a day, most of them flown by Air Force U-2s under the control of the Strategic Air Command (SAC).

On October 14, an Air Force U-2 of the 4080th Strategic Reconnaissance Wing, flown from McCoy Air Force Base, Florida, by Major Steve Heyser, brought back the first photos of SS-4s in Cuba. They were spotted near San Cristóbal, fifty miles southwest of Havana. Other U-2s returned with photographs of forty Il-28 bombers, aircraft capable of delivering nuclear weapons, parked on Cuban airfields. The Soviets apparently had hoped to install these offensive weapons covertly, behind a shield of SAMs, and present the United States with a *fait accompli*, but the plan had been foiled by America's high-flying reconnaissance pilots. Their achievement was not without cost, however. On October 27, Major Rudolf Anderson, flying over the Cuban naval base at Banes, was killed when his U-2 was struck by an SA-2. This missile was later reported to have been fired by Cuban leader Fidel Castro himself, who, while visiting the site, asked how he could shoot down the U-2 that

A picture taken by a U-2 flying 70,000 feet above Cuba shows a nascent launch site for Soviet SS-4 medium-range ballistic missiles. In addition to trailers for transporting the weapons, the photograph shows erectors used to launch them—as well as assorted vehicles and a tent city set up to shelter technicians and other workers.

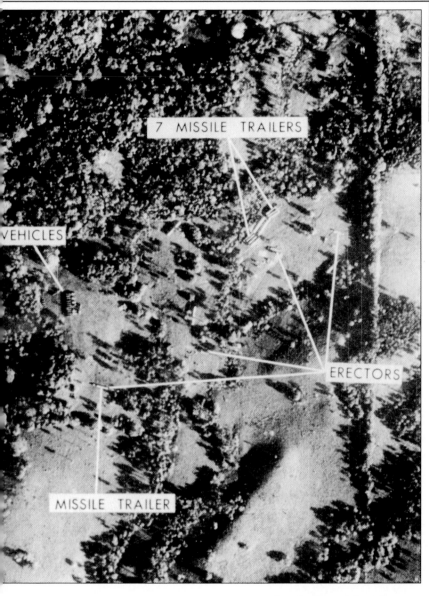

7 MISSILE TRAILERS

VEHICLES

ERECTORS

MISSILE TRAILER

had appeared on the radarscope. An officer pointed to the firing button, and to the astonishment of the assembly, Castro pushed it.

When he received the hard evidence of the Soviet Union's new and dangerous offensive capabilities in Cuba, President Kennedy went public, initiating a naval blockade of Cuba and demanding an immediate withdrawal of Soviet ballistic missiles and bombers. In the tautest confrontation of the Cold War, the United States and the Soviet Union were, in the words of Defense Secretary Robert McNamara, eyeball-to-eyeball. Finally, Khrushchev blinked, agreeing to withdraw the SS-4s and Il-28s. In return, the United States consented to remove its Jupiter intermediate-range nuclear missiles from Turkey. Supplemented by low-flying RF-101s and RF-8 Crusaders (Navy reconnaissance jets), U-2s monitored the Soviet pullout and photographed the SS-4s in open crates on the decks of freighters as they sailed home. The crisis was over.

Kelly Johnson's remarkable spyplanes also served elsewhere. Stationed at Bien Hoa Air Base in Vietnam, they photographed military and industrial targets in North Vietnam that later ended up on target lists for Operation Rolling Thunder and Operation Linebacker, the extended air offensives against the North. But as the war progressed, the North Vietnamese beefed up their air defenses, bringing an end to U-2 flights over Hanoi and Haiphong by installing improved SA-2s in considerable numbers around those cities. And in a case possibly unique in the annals of aerial reconnaissance—the parties under surveillance have given their blessing to U-2 overflights. Under the provisions of the Camp David Accord, which regulates Egyptian and Israeli forces along their common border, U-2s provide photographic coverage of the Sinai to assist peacekeeping observers on the ground.

51

The latest version of the ubiquitous high flier entered service in 1981 as the TR-1. Besides cameras and a suite of electronic-countermeasures gear to protect it against surface-to-air missiles, the TR-1 carries an advanced synthetic-aperture radar system (ASARS) that can look sideways across an adversary's border to scan a swath of territory more than 100 miles wide, day or night, clear skies or cloudy. The TR-1 can even provide a live picture of a battlefield for ground commanders. During the Gulf War, an on-board electro-optical imaging system transmitted pictures from the plane to ground stations in near-real time. "The sensors are state of the art," said Colonel Thomas Keck, commander of the Ninth SRW, "and the sensors are what will keep this a viable platform well into the twenty-first century."

The Untouchable Blackbird

Three years before Soviet missileers shot down Gary Powers, the CIA's Richard Bissell had foreseen the possibility of such an occurrence. "I came to the conclusion that we should start working on the successor to the U-2," he said, "because it was clear to me that sooner or later the U-2 would be vulnerable to interception." Once again, the project—code-named Oxcart—was given to Lockheed's famed Skunk Works under Kelly Johnson. His team set out to design a plane that would fly higher and faster than the U-2 and be less visible to radar.

In a strategy later dubbed

the stealth approach to designing aircraft, Johnson's team was to reduce insofar as possible the radar cross section of the aircraft by eliminating right angles and large flat surfaces that are such effective reflectors of radar beams. A SAM battery could not shoot down what it could not see and, without a radar lock, the missiles were effectively blind. But stealth alone would not be a complete defense; the new plane would also need the capability to outrun anything thrown at it. An SA-2, for example, required about ninety seconds to climb to spyplane altitude. If a reconnaissance aircraft could fly fast enough, given the limited range of fire-control radar, it could beat the missile to the intercept point, leaving the

Successor to the U-2, the Lockheed TR-1A has an enormous wingspan of 103 feet that allows the plane to fly as high as 90,000 feet, above 99 percent of earth's atmosphere. Torpedo-shaped pods on the wings are fuel tanks and sensor pods; reconnaissance sensors reside in the plane's long snout and in the fuselage. Lockheed painted the TR-1 black both to reduce the plane's visibility against the sky—it too is black at such altitudes—and to absorb enemy radar waves.

SAM unable to execute the high-G turn necessary to follow. To be assured of accomplishing this feat, Johnson calculated, a plane would have to fly faster than three times the speed of sound. The world's first mach 3-plus airplane was about to appear.

In its final form, the Skunk Works' creation—bearing the Lockheed designation A-12—was an impressive machine. A long, sleek fuselage with a pointed nose stretched back to delta wings, each mounting a huge engine, above which was a vertical stabilizer canted slightly inward to reduce the radar cross section. A special radar-absorbing, heat-resistant paint covered the exterior. Black in color, this paint not only made the airplane harder to see at the edge of the atmosphere where it flew but also furnished its popular moniker—Blackbird.

On April 26, 1962, the first A-12 screamed aloft from Groom Lake, flown by test pilot Lou Schalk dressed in a spacesuit similar to those worn by astronauts. Extensive performance tests proved that the aircraft could do everything its sponsors wanted and Johnson had promised. Of the twelve single-seat A-12 reconnaissance aircraft built for the CIA, about half were lost to operational and training accidents over the next several years; the remainder were cannibalized for spare parts.

The Strategic Air Command, meanwhile, was looking for a superfast high-flying recon plane to supplement its own U-2s. The end result, produced in collaboration with the CIA, was a modified version of the A-12 having larger dimensions to carry more fuel and to provide room for sensors and a second cockpit behind the pilot for a reconnaissance systems officer (RSO).

On July 24, 1964, President Lyndon Johnson held a press conference to announce the "successful development of a major new strategic manned aircraft system [for] the Strategic Air Command." He went on to say: "This system employs the new SR-71 aircraft." Actually, "SR-71" was a slip of the presidential tongue; the aircraft had been designated the RS-71, for Reconnaissance/Strike. But the

SR-71 Blackbirds come together on the assembly line at Lockheed's secret Skunk Works facility in Palmdale, California. A sign atop the foreman's shed reminds workers not to cause foreign object damage by leaving tools where they might be sealed inside partly completed aircraft, for example.

Air Force brass deemed it more prudent to rechristen the plane SR-71—for Strategic Reconnaissance—than confront the president with his gaffe. Johnson was accurate, however, in describing the new plane's performance: "The aircraft will fly at more than three times the speed of sound and operate at altitudes in excess of 80,000 feet. It will use the most advanced observation equipment in the world." And for all the confusion over its official designation, the SR-71 kept the nickname Blackbird.

The maiden flight took place at Palmdale, California, on December 22, 1964. Eighteen months later, SR-71s were operational with SAC's Ninth Strategic Reconnaissance Wing at Beale Air Force Base, California. Other Blackbirds were deployed to bases on Okinawa and in England. From there, they undertook top-secret missions the world over. The flights always involved a lone aircraft and were scheduled irregularly to increase the likelihood of surprise. Often, the plane was in and out before the other side could react.

No SR-71 has ever flown directly over the Soviet Union, though they have often passed offshore. The USSR claims that its dominion over the skies extends twelve miles beyond its coastline; the United States recognizes a three-mile limit. This difference of opinion became the source of a diplomatic protest from the Soviets virtually every time an SR-71 crossed the twelve-mile line. On occasion, when conditions seemed favorable for an intercept, fighters would be dispatched in an effort to shoot down an SR-71. None succeeded. Pilot Viktor I. Belenko, who defected to Japan with a MiG-25 Foxbat in 1976, described the futility of trying to intercept SR-71s along the Siberian coast and never being able to close with them. Even with missiles that could reach above the MiG-25's 78,000-foot ceiling to 88,500 feet, the chase always proved fruitless. "Even if we could reach it, our missiles lack the velocity to overtake the SR-71 if they are fired in a tail chase. And if they are fired head-on, their guidance systems cannot adjust quickly enough to the high closing speed." Although some Blackbirds have crashed because of mechanical failure or pilot error, none has ever been shot down by enemy fire.

For the handful of pilots and RSOs who flew the SR-71, the experience was unique. "It may look like a fighter, but it didn't fly like a fighter," said Major Terry Pappas, a Blackbird pilot for four and a half years. The plane's sleek lines belied the fact that it was as large as a DC-9 airliner. With its blazing speed, there was no question of last-second adjustments over the target; the radius of the tightest turn possible at top speed without losing altitude was 99.5 miles. Many pilots speak of the SR-71 as being a "cerebral" airplane to fly. When "you're doing thirty-three miles a minute," said Lieutenant Colonel Jerry Glasser, another SR-71 driver, "you're basically thinking about four hundred miles ahead of the airplane—twelve to thirteen minutes ahead. And while you don't have to be fast, you have to be right the first time."

The plane traveled twice as fast as the earth turns. Colonel Glasser once took off after nightfall from Beale Air Force Base bound for Okinawa. Over the Pacific, he caught up with the sun and watched as it appeared to rise in the west. Turning his aircraft south, he flew until it was again shrouded in darkness, then resumed his original heading—and watched a second sunrise. As embellishment to the apparent paradox, the phenomenon offered a colorful vista. "You're seeing the sun rise and set through the entire atmosphere," said Major Pappas. "You get either maximum refraction and filtering of the sun's rays or you get the absolute minimum.

There's a tremendous range of brightness and color. In fact, as you go through the transition from daylight to darkness, you do it so rapidly we called it 'the terminator.' It's like going through a wall—into a black hole, almost."

Blackbirds flew for twenty-four years, ultimately succumbing to changing intelligence priorities and budgetary constraints. It is true that the SR-71 was the world's most expensive airplane to operate and maintain—$85,000 per hour of flying time. Ground crews spent forty hours going over the Blackbird for every hour it spent aloft. Even the minor things that went into it were expensive. Skunk Works head Ben Rich joked that the SR-71 was the only airplane with oil that cost more than Scotch whisky.

On March 27, 1990, the last operational Air Force SR-71 (three were loaned to the National Aeronautics and Space Administration for aerodynamic research) flew from Beale to the Air Force Museum at Wright-Patterson Air Force Base in Dayton, Ohio. "It just doesn't seem like a museum piece," said Lieutenant Colonel Gil Luloff, a former SR-71 pilot. "You take something that cosmic, that capable and still on top of the list record-wise, and put it in a museum. It's kind of a dichotomy." Perhaps so, but by the late 1980s, another strategic reconnaissance vehicle had matured to the point that the Blackbird's services were not only uneconomical, they were no longer absolutely necessary.

The Ultimate Vantage Point

Soon after the end of World War II, the U.S. military—with technical assistance from German scientists who only months earlier had been working for Hitler—turned its attention to the practicality of rocket-launched earth satellites. In the spring of 1946, a private think tank, called Project RAND (for Research and Development), was commissioned to prepare a feasibility study. In addition to examining the myriad technological challenges that a space program would offer, the study also described its potential applications. Among the proposals shone one noting that "the satellite offers an observation aircraft that cannot be brought down by an enemy who has not mastered similar techniques."

A second assessment by RAND, issued the following year, specifically addressed the concept of reconnaissance satellites and concluded, in part, that, "by installing television equipment combined with one or more telescopes in a satellite, an observation and reconnaissance tool without parallel could be established. A spaceship can be placed upon an oblique or north-south orbit so as to cover the entire surface of the earth at frequent intervals as the earth rotates beneath the orbit."

In September 1947, the Air Force developed a keen interest in RAND's theoretical postulations. The idea of real-time imagery on a global scale had great appeal to a service whose mandate in the event of war included both striking strategic targets within the Soviet Union and protecting the United States from surprise attack. Over the next ten years, while the United States and the Soviet Union engaged in a nuclear-arms race and developed new means of delivering those weapons, the Air Force chartered additional ruminations from RAND.

In the mid-1950s, the television idea became one of three concepts considered for a practical satellite reconnaissance system. A second proposal suggested a satellite equipped with a regular high-altitude camera that used self-developing film devised by Edwin Land, founder of the Polaroid Corporation. After a picture was taken, it would be developed in orbit, then scanned for electronic transmission to earth. The third scheme envisioned a space vehicle carrying a camera that would take pictures until film ran out, then the satellite would return the exposed film for processing.

Known as the recoverable-film method, the third candidate offered the best resolution, but it lost out because of the difficulties projected in returning the payload to earth without incinerating it. To shield the film from the tremendous temperatures of reentry into the atmosphere, the proposal called for a mass of copper to absorb the heat generated by friction with the air. The weight of the copper was so great, however, that adding to the satellite a camera and film sufficient to make the project worth the effort would have overtaxed available rockets, making it impossible to loft the vehicle into a suitable orbit.

Both of the other satellite concepts sidestepped this problem by returning images electronically. Surveillance by television had the advantage of being simpler than developing film and scanning it, but the poor resolution offered by video technology of the era decided the matter in favor of the scanned-image technique. The Air Force called the program SAMOS. It would be the next best thing to a live television picture, and with Russian ICBMs that could reach U.S. cities a half hour after launch under development, the idea of an Air Force general sitting before a bank of screens and monitoring events at Soviet missile sites had great appeal.

SAMOS would eventually launch ten satellites, but almost before the ink had dried on the contract to produce them, two events occurred. In October 1957, the Soviets shocked America with the successful launching of Sputnik. No other event could have given more impetus to the U.S. satellite program. Funding was quadrupled overnight, and the space race was on. Second, a new way had evolved to insulate a satellite payload returning from orbit. Called the ablative-shield method, it used relatively lightweight plastic that would gradually vaporize, dissipating heat in the process. The extra funding and the plastic heat shield for the satellite opened the gate for Project Corona—recoverable-film satellites to be developed under the auspices of the CIA.

Project Corona bore the scientific cover name Discoverer. Inside each space vehicle was a panoramic camera with a pivoting lens, a high-resolution device that had been designed several years earlier to take pictures from high-altitude balloons. To retrieve the photographs, the program counted on a complicated procedure. As Discoverer sailed over Alaska on a southerly course toward Hawaii, a capsule full of exposed film would be detached from the satellite. A small retrorocket would then slow the package for reentry into the atmosphere. At 50,000 feet, a parachute would pop open and a radio beacon in the capsule would switch on. Several Air Force C-119 Flying Boxcars—twin-engine, twin-tail-boom cargo planes—would circle the recovery area. From the open rear cargo door, each C-119 trailed two long, rigid bars connected by nylon ropes. By steering toward the parachute, the pilot hoped to snag it in midair, thus permitting the crew to reel in the capsule.

Such was the theory, but the program seemed jinxed from the start. On February 28, 1959, Discoverer I achieved orbit but tumbled out of control after its stabilizing system failed. Discoverer II ejected the capsule at the wrong time, and it missed the recovery area completely, never to be found. The next two launches failed to attain orbit. Discoverer V ejected the capsule at the right time, but then it was never seen or heard from again. And so it went, a procession of failures that took months to pass by.

Finally, on August 10, 1960—and not much more than three

months after Gary Powers's U-2 was shot down—Discoverer XIII performed exactly as intended. But the C-119 catchplane missed the capsule, which splashed into the sea. Navy frogmen, dispatched by helicopter, eventually made the recovery, the first of a man-made object returning from orbit. The Soviets were certainly able to track the Discoverer satellites as they passed repeatedly overhead. Wary of further provoking them in the wake of the Powers incident, the Air Force, which spoke for the project instead of the ultrareticent CIA, announced that Discoverer XIII was a "diagnostic test" of the spacecraft's telemetry system and the as yet unproven capsule recovery method.

Eight days later Discoverer XIV performed flawlessly and the capsule was successfully snagged in flight by a C-119. Previous Discoverer flights had been widely publicized, but that policy changed almost overnight with the success of the fourteenth mission; Air Force press releases spoke only of an "eighty-four-pound instrumented capsule." The government put an airtight lid of secrecy on the U.S. satellite program. SAMOS officially ceased to exist while still under way, and the more widely known Discoverer program was eased out of the public eye.

In reality, Discoverer XIV had successfully photographed a Russian airfield at Mys Schmidta as well as an ICBM base at Plesetsk, which, ironically, had also been the target of Gary Powers's ill-fated U-2 flight. Soon after the film had been plucked from the air, it was eagerly being examined by CIA analysts, the first photo interpreters ever to compile a report based on pictures taken from earth orbit.

Six days after Discoverer XIV's return, a high-level meeting took place at the White House. After examining the satellite's handiwork, President Eisenhower addressed proposals for administering the suddenly successful space reconnaissance program. The result was the birth of a new government agency, the National Reconnaissance Office (NRO). The Air Force and the CIA would continue to run their own programs, but henceforth the overall direction of satellite reconnaissance would be vested in the NRO. Under the cover name Office of Missile and Satellite Systems—later changed to Office of Space Systems—the supersecretive NRO took up residence in the Pentagon. Though the organization controls a budget of three to four billion dollars a year, the executive branch has never officially acknowledged its existence. And though the Air Force, as the owner of the launch vehicles and a primary customer for the

A C-119 Flying Boxcar succeeds in practice at bagging a payload similar in weight to the film capsule of a Discoverer photo-reconnaissance satellite, shown being fitted to the nose of a rocket booster in the inset. The maneuver required the pilot to fly just above the parachute supporting the satellite and snare the canopy with a trapezelike apparatus hanging below the aircraft. Crewmen then reeled their catch aboard the plane.

intelligence data, plays a major role, both the director of the NRO and his deputy come from the civilian rather than the uniformed side of the Department of Defense.

Despite official reticence about Discoverer—"no comment" had become the official word on the program—it is certain that, by the summer of 1961, Discoverer satellites were routinely providing high-quality photos of the Soviet Union. Each spacecraft cut a wide swath across the Soviet Union and "bucket dropped" imagery that quickly had a sensational impact in Washington. On the flimsiest of information in a worst-case state of mind, Air Force intelligence analysts had estimated that the Soviets would deploy as many as 700 Soviet ICBMs by 1963, far more than the United States would possess. The CIA predicted only 400 missiles in operation by then, a smaller figure than the Air Force's but still a significant number. But the Discoverer photographs shown to President Kennedy in 1961 revealed no more than twenty-five Soviet ICBMs in service and offered no evidence of a crash program to field the vast numbers of ICBMs foretold by the experts.

Soviet propagandists hotly criticized the United States for its Discoverer program, but the ruckus died down after the USSR's launch of its first reconnaissance satellite in April 1962. With an equilibrium of sorts reached in space technology, Eisenhower's Open Skies became a reality.

With both parties' tacit approval, the United States and the Soviet Union forged ahead in the field of spy satellites as rapidly as technology permitted. Launches became routine, the earlier string of failures forgotten. Discoverer was soon obsolete.

On June 28, 1962, the CIA launched a new satellite designated the Keyhole Four, or KH-4. Only a handful of these vehicles were launched before they were replaced by the KH-4A. This satellite boasted a wide-area camera having a resolution of ten feet and designed to take broad panoramas that might detect changes or new developments in Soviet military activity. In addition, it was probably the first photint satellite to carry two film capsules. The KH-4As ran out of film after approximately twenty-three days in orbit, so a replacement was sent up almost once a month. After three and a half years, the KH-4A was succeeded by the KH-4B, which offered improved photographic resolution and also carried eighteen small thrusters that allowed the satellite to change altitude in orbit. Of the eighty-five KH-4As and KH-4Bs sent aloft between 1963 and 1972, only six failed.

Meanwhile, the Air Force had recognized that real-time imagery from satellites remained beyond the reach of technology, while the recoverable-capsule method had been proved. Thus its own second-generation satellite, the KH-7, was a bucket dropper in the Discoverer tradition. Of the thirty-eight launched between 1963 and 1967, thirty-six were successful. Increased friction with the atmosphere—the result of an orbit lower than the one flown by the CIA Keyholes—cut average lifetime to only five and a half days, but being closer to earth allowed the satellite, equipped with longer focal length cameras, to pick up objects only eighteen inches across. The KH-4A and KH-7 worked as a team coordinated through the NRO, with the Air Force satellites taking a closer look at suspicious features identified earlier in the smaller-scale, wider-area pictures taken by the KH-4As.

To pair up with the improved KH-4B, the Air Force launched the first of the 100 percent successful KH-8 series in July 1966. On average, the KH-8's life in low orbit was six times longer than the KH-7's, possibly because the new satellite was more streamlined or because, after sinking to lower altitude, it could get a boost from its thrusters to a higher one. Toward the end of its eighteen years in service—the longest of any spy satellite—refinements in the KH-8s' cameras had produced a resolution of a mere six inches.

The KH-9 "Big Bird" program started in 1971. As large as a Greyhound bus and weighing 30,000 pounds, the Big Bird satellite carried a special camera designed to take surveillance images of immense areas—nearly 30,000 square miles. Like Discoverer and the previous Keyhole satellites, the photos were parachuted to earth in film-return pods. Each Big Bird, however, carried four pods instead of two. With its huge ground swath, Big Bird was an incomparable tool for intelligence analysts, who loudly lamented the satellite's demise in 1984 after nineteen successful launches.

Big Bird imagery or supplemental, close-in photographs provided by a continuing succession of KH-8 satellites were retrieved from space every three weeks or so, on average. While this schedule provided employment for a considerable number of photo interpreters, it did not satisfy the Air Force's desire for instant pictures, a goal that the service had continued working toward for some twenty years since SAMOS.

Success came in 1976, while the Big Bird program was still going strong, with the first KH-11 satellite, code-named Kennan. Replacing photographic film behind the huge lens of its camera was a new light-sensitive instrument called a charge-coupled device (CCD). Invented by Bell Labs in 1969, a CCD is made of silicon no different from that used in memory chips for computers. This material, in addition to its other remarkable properties, converts light into an electrical charge according to brightness. Extremely sensitive, silicon can detect virtually every photon of light that strikes it. To make a CCD, the surface of a silicon chip no larger than a postage stamp is divided into a grid containing perhaps 640,000 tiny squares called picture elements, or pixels, each of them recording a fragment of the image as focused by the satellite's telescopic lens. Such arrays can be clustered together to provide larger areas of "film" that produces images of exceptional clarity.

As soon as the CCD is exposed to make an image, the charge in each pixel is measured and given a number that represents its position in the grid and its charge, which corresponds to brightness. Easily transmitted by radio without error to earth, these numbers are used to generate a picture either on film or on a computer monitor. If necessary, a photo interpreter can be looking at what the satellite saw only seconds earlier. Real-time satellite imagery had become a reality.

The Kennan had other important advantages over its predecessors. Earlier satellites could change altitude. But as long as its 6,500 pounds of fuel lasted, this newest Keyhole could also change the angle of its orbit with the equator, altering its ground track to photograph different targets on succeeding passes. Besides looking

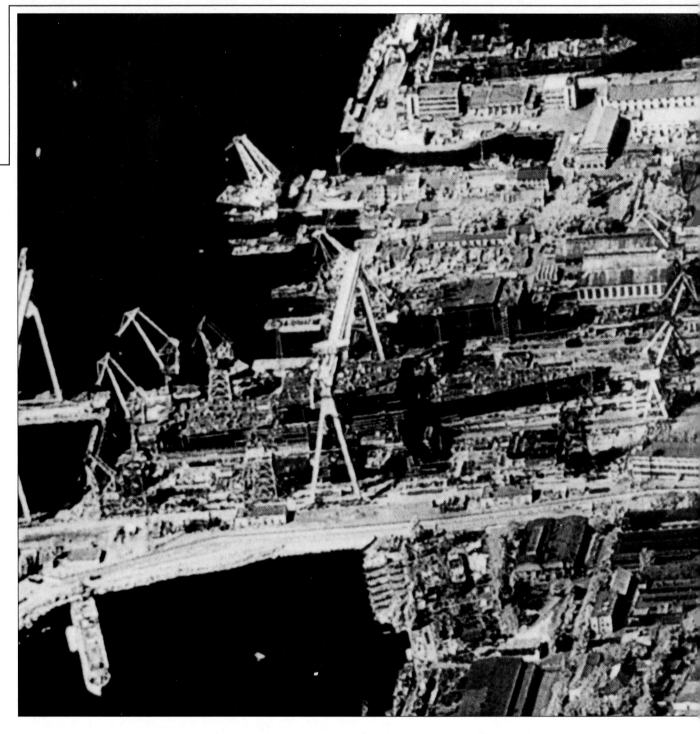

straight down, it could peer more than 350 miles forward or to either side of its course. These capabilities vastly extended its view on each pass across the USSR—and complicated the Soviets' job of concealing their activities, should they wish to do so. Even so, the patch of ground covered by the KH-11 when looking straight down—a matter of only a few square miles—was (and remains) a small fraction of the area seen by Big Bird. Consequently, several CCD images are often pieced together in a mosaic.

Keeping the capabilities of spy satellites a secret is a top priority, for to reveal them is to warn surveillance targets about how much

Illegally released to the public in 1984, this KH-11 photograph shows the Soviets' first full-size aircraft carrier abuilding at the Nikolaev Shipyard on the Black Sea. Bow and stern sections, constructed separately under a huge gantry, were later welded together to complete the ship. From such photographs (the originals, no longer available, showed more detail than this version) analysts judged that the ship would have two aircraft elevators, three steam catapults, and the ability to hold up to seventy-five planes.

might be known of their activities. Regardless of the tight security around such programs in the United States and other countries, information sometimes gets out. Less than a year after the launch of the first KH-11, William Kampiles, a twenty-two-year-old watch officer in the CIA's operations center, became disillusioned with his job. He had found none of the intrigue and adventure he had anticipated when he started working for the CIA. The high point of his day was gathering classified refuse, crumpling it into paper bags, and delivering them down the hall to the incinerator chute. After only eight months with the agency and a formal evaluation indicating an unsatisfactory performance, Kampiles resigned—but not before stealing a copy of the operating manual for the Kennan satellite.

In February 1978, the newly minted spy traveled to Greece and sold the manual to a military attaché at the Soviet embassy for three thousand dollars. Upon return to the United States, Kampiles began boasting to friends of his escapade and sought a job at the CIA as a double agent. Instead, the spy's foray into the real world of secret agents netted him forty years in a federal penitentiary, but the Soviets received an intelligence windfall. They learned the true excellence of the images that the KH-11 could provide and how much of the USSR's military activities it could see. But even with that information, there was little the Soviets could do to counter the capabilities of the satellite. By passing over the Soviet Union four times a day, twice during daylight, the KH-11s discovered the deployment of mobile SS-25 missiles and railcar-mounted SS-24s, both ten-warhead ICBMs. The satellites also spotted the introduction of the supersonic Blackjack bomber and construction of the first full-size Soviet aircraft carrier.

After the Kampiles affair came to light, the government inventoried the KH-11 manuals and discovered that seventeen others were missing. Two turned up later, but the remainder are still unaccounted for. Some feared that, with the information in the pilfered manual, the Soviets would be able to build their own KH-11; as far as anyone knew, they were still in the photographic film era of spy satellites. But a longtime member of the U.S. intelligence community discounted this theory; reading the owner's manual to a car will tell you how it works, he said, but not how to build one.

On August 8, 1989, an improved KH-11—known as the Advanced Kennan—went into orbit aboard the space shuttle *Columbia*. This larger version of the satellite is sixty-four feet long and carries half its empty weight—15,000 pounds—in maneuvering fuel, which permits the satellite to descend for a closeup photo pass and then to boost itself upward again. Because of this capability, some observers believe that the Advanced Kennan might even be able to dodge antisatellite weapons that the Soviets have been credited with developing. Along with the customary visual-spectrum camera, the Advanced Kennan has an infrared system that produces digital imagery from heat produced by objects on the ground. This capability is useful in daylight—penetrating smoke, revealing the presence of camouflage, and showing which planes on an airfield have recently run their engines, for example—and also gives the satellite true night-imaging capability from space. Additionally, the new KH-11 can produce precise contour maps for use by cruise missiles to find their way to the target.

Yet for all its features, the advanced KH-11 could not see through clouds, a blindness that limits the usefulness of a spy satellite in areas such as Europe and the western USSR, where the skies are overcast 70 percent of the time. As it happens, this form of satellite sightlessness had become much less troublesome by the time of the Advanced Kennan. In the preceding year, 1988, a new system, code-named Lacrosse, was carried aloft in the cargo bay of the space shuttle *Atlantis*. Once stabilized in orbit, the Lacrosse deployed a huge rectangular radar antenna. Used conventionally to flash pulses of radar energy toward earth and record their echoes, the antenna would produce images so blurry as to be totally uninformative to interpreters trying to puzzle them out. However, by mimicking a much larger antenna through a computerized approach to radar imaging called synthetic-aperture radar *(pages 67-70)*, Lacrosse can

Radar Cameras

Somewhere in the world, a crisis swiftly unfolds. Hungry for information, military leaders impatiently await fresh images from a photographic satellite that is about to pass over the area. But all of the miraculous technology packed in that spacecraft 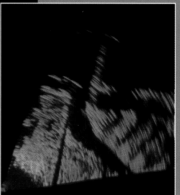 may be as useless as so much scrap metal if a bank of clouds drifts between its probing lens and the target. Now, however, a new generation of orbiting spies defeats not only foul weather but darkness and smoke as well through the use of radar.

This electronic marvel developed in the 1940s measures the distances to objects by emitting pulses of radio waves and timing how long it takes for echoes to arrive at the antenna. The radar determines the objects' bearing by noting the direction of the echoes. Range and bearing information, appearing as blips of light on a screen, compose a fuzzy picture of the scene.

The image shown here—a barely decipherable likeness of a marina on an inlet—is testimony to the poor resolving power of traditional radar systems. The image consists of rectangles known as resolution cells. Incapable of reproducing details smaller than their own dimensions, the cells account for the indistinctness of the picture. To shrink the resolution cells—and thereby improve the quality of the image—electronics engineers turn to a technique called synthetic-aperture radar *(overleaf)*.

botprint of a SAR sat-
rs a wide swath on
hes within the strip,
ps fifty square feet
ere as oversize rectan-
ye and then reflect
ry radar pulse. The
es the echoes, classi-
according to Doppler
ed to the ground and
h facts about the sat-
it, this data permits a
to assign each bit of
nifted echo from rec-
the ground to the ap-
esolution cell in the
ardless of spacecraft
low bright each area
the final image de-
he average intensity
es it produces.

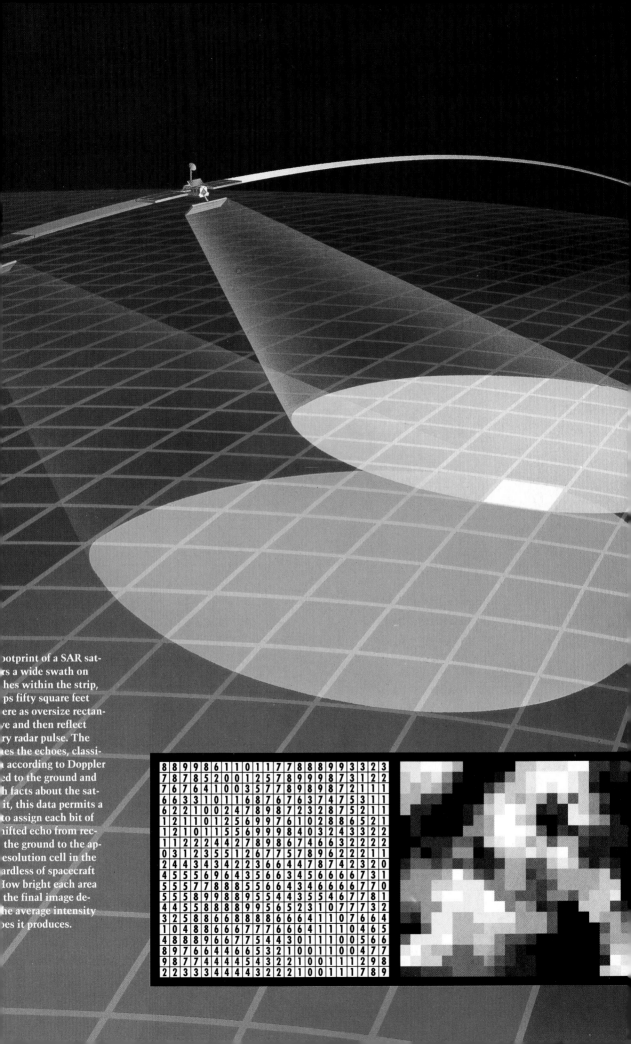

A Stratagem for a Sharp Image

Radar is a much more precise gauge of range than of bearing, but to produce a clear picture, a radar imaging system must be able to measure both. Improved bearing resolution can be obtained by increasing the size of the antenna, or aperture as it is sometimes called. A radar having bearing perception as acute as its range-finding ability would require an antenna ranging from hundreds of feet to thousands of feet in length, depending on altitude.

Enter synthetic-aperture radar, or SAR, in which a big antenna is simulated by a smaller one. As such an antenna moves along a straight line, transmitting all the while, resolution can be made to equal that of a much larger structure. One ingredient that is crucial to the process is the Doppler effect *(right)*, which accounts for the difference in tone of a train whistle when the train is approaching or receding. Another is a powerful computer used to collate into a single, high-resolution image all the many thousands of low-resolution snapshots taken by the moving radar.

Early SARs were mounted in aircraft; the SR-71 Blackbird, the U-2 and the TR-1, the RC-135, and others all had them. The radars took in an oblique view of the ground that permitted spyplanes to look several dozen miles into an adversary's territory from a vantage point across the border. SAR's sidelong glance also maximizes range resolution by emphasizing, from the aircraft's vantage point, the difference in distance between adjacent points on the ground. For this reason, SAR satellites such as Lacrosse are also sideways lookers even though they are able to fly unimpeded directly over any spot on the globe.

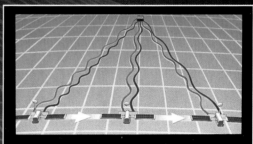

A SAR system transmits at a constant frequency *(blue)*. Because of the Doppler effect, however, the echo frequency *(red)* becomes higher as the satellite approaches a target and lower as it moves away. Directly opposite the target, the two frequencies are equal.

In order to create a picture, a SAR computer assigns to every resolution cell in the image a numerical value that represents the brightness of the corresponding patch of ground *(far left)*. For the sake of simplicity, only 10 numbers are shown here instead of the 256 values commonly used in digital images. The computer then "paints by the numbers," applying a different shade of gray for each brightness value *(center)*. At left is a magnified section of an actual SAR image that samples the full palette of grays.

The World through SAR Eyes

A synthetic-aperture radar image seems at once familiar and alien—somewhat like a photographic negative of a scene that is lit by a flashbulb, yet different. Some reasons for the disparity result from computer manipulation of the image. Others, however, derive from the nature of radar; hundreds of such differences account for the character of the image.

Some substances opaque to light are transparent to radar beams because of their longer wavelength, explaining why a tank successfully camouflaged from a camera, for example, stands out brightly to radar.

Horizontal, untextured surfaces tend to return little radar energy toward the antenna. Thus a concrete parking lot, for example, appears much darker in a SAR image than in a photo. Similarly, textured surfaces tend to appear bright in a radar image. A collection of buildings or other man-made objects stands out especially well because right angles, which abound in such contexts, are superior reflectors of radar.

Runways in this SAR image of an airfield appear dark because of a lack of texture, revealing a row of four parked aircraft (1). Vegetation is darker in the foreground than in the background, where the radar's angle of view makes it appear more textured. Most clearly visible are angular metallic objects such as hangars (2) and oil tanks (3).

distinguish objects and terrain features as small as three feet across, performance that far exceeds photographs taken by first-generation spy satellites like the early Discoverers.

Lacrosse could see more sharply still, if it were not for an electronic bottleneck at a communications satellite called TDRSS (Tracking and Data Relay Satellite System), which is used for relaying data to earth as streams of ones and zeros called bits, the language of the digital computers on the ground that actually create the Lacrosse image. TDRSS can relay data no faster than 300 million bits per second (BPS), sufficient for three-foot resolution. Lacrosse generates data at a rate of billions of bits per second, the foundation for one-foot resolution when TDRSS can handle the flow. "The data rate limits everything," noted a satellite engineer at NASA's Jet Propulsion Laboratory, "resolution, gray-scale accuracy, and field of view." An advanced TDRSS, the first of four anticipated, went into orbit on August 2, 1991. When the other three are in position, improved Lacrosse images will be available from every point in the satellite's orbit.

Soon, anything of consequence that appears on earth's surface will be visible from space. And while computers working with the digital images provided by modern overhead surveillance systems can greatly assist interpreters in some aspects of their work *(pages 76-85)*, they must still be able to identify what they see in the pictures, a task that is often purposely complicated by an adversary.

Camouflage and deception are longstanding defenses against observation from above. Mock-ups of military equipment, such as full-size plastic or inflatable rubber tanks and fiberglass airplanes and missile launchers, are placed to mislead photo interpreters. Bomb craters can be painted on runways and holes simulated on rooftops to mimic bomb damage that never occurred or that has been repaired. Entire airfields and industrial areas have been tinted to look like rural settings from above.

Yet even when there can be no doubt as to the identity of objects on the ground, there can remain a great deal of uncertainty about their significance. For this reason, photographic intelligence is sometimes of frustratingly little value when considered apart from other information about the import of the observations. Just such an issue arose on the eve of Iraq's 1990 invasion of Kuwait.

Under Watchful Eyes

Arcing through space in an elliptical polar orbit, a KH-11 photore-connaissance satellite swept over the Persian Gulf in late July 1990. Responding to ground commands, the huge vehicle focused its electro-optical imaging system on the deserts of Iraq, Kuwait, and Saudi Arabia. The high-resolution sensors easily captured the spectacle unfolding 160 miles below. On the Iraq-Kuwait border had massed a horde of Iraqi tanks and armored personnel carriers, along with more than 100,000 troops. Behind them stretched truck convoys, artillery pieces, and other support elements—all the sinews of war. The KH-11 recorded the scene, sending its images digitally via relay satellite to Fort Belvoir, Virginia. There, the electronic pulses were decoded, processed, and converted into photographic prints for distribution within the U.S. intelligence community.

Analysts and photo interpreters who examined the KH-11's handiwork knew of Iraqi dictator Saddam Hussein's longstanding claim that the emirate of Kuwait was an Iraqi province severed in the partition of the Ottoman Empire after World War I. Since then, Iraqi forces had assembled along Kuwait's border on two occasions, when a dispute of some kind had erupted, but they had always stopped short of invasion. The present quarrel, which concerned oil production, rights to an oil field that straddled their common border, and the settlement of war debts incurred by the Iraqis during a recent conflict with Iran, seemed no more serious than the others, and the consensus among the analysts, who customarily offer the most pessimistic predictions to avoid being caught short, was that Iraq intended the show of force as a bluff to pressure Kuwait.

Such intimidation works best if the victim believes the threat. Saddam might have settled for moving some tanks to the border and leaving most of the other men and matériel in garrison, but with satellites watching every move, the maneuver would have been seen for what it was—nothing more than saber rattling staged for dramatic effect. For his scheme to appear credible, it had to be consistent, in every detail, with preparations for a real invasion.

And so it was. At 2:00 a.m. on August 2, Iraqi tanks rumbled across the border and raced toward Kuwait City. In less than a day—before the United States could respond—Kuwait was overrun.

The question then became what would Saddam do next. The

KH-11 continued its passes over the gulf area, relaying images of Iraqi armored columns streaming south toward Kuwait's border with Saudi Arabia. Taken aback by Saddam's blatant aggression, U.S. leaders vowed not to underestimate his ambitions again. When the satellite showed his forces digging in along the Saudi border, the United States decided to take no chances. In no time at all, the Iraqi army could move from its ostensibly defensive posture, aimed at protecting its gains in Kuwait, to an offensive one. If Iraq were to capture the oil fields of Saudi Arabia, Saddam would control 40 percent of the world's oil reserves, an intolerable situation.

Within days, U.S. forces were on the way to Saudi Arabia, at first to prevent Iraq from entering Saudi Arabia and later, in concert with the armed might of many nations, to eject the aggressor from Kuwait. As the deployments began, American intelligence agencies concentrated their assets on the area. By mid-January 1991, when the final ultimatum for Iraqi withdrawal from Kuwait expired and the U.S.-led coalition was poised for an offensive war, every acre of the potential battlefield and every visible sign of Iraqi military presence had been monitored, photographed, scanned, mapped, and plotted. Of great importance to the looming air campaign, the Advanced Kennan provided terrain contour maps for the Navy's cruise missiles to be used against heavily defended Iraqi targets.

At no time in the history of warfare had such a massive amount of intelligence been afforded a commander prior to battle. The Gulf War was watched by more satellites than any previous conflict. Up to half a dozen KH-11s were maneuvered in orbit so that one could pass directly over the Persian Gulf every two days. The Lacrosse joined in and bounced imagery off the TDRSS both day and night.

War began with an air campaign. Later, General Norman Schwarzkopf, operational commander in the gulf, would complain to Congress about the equivocal analysis that he received from U.S. intelligence agencies. Nonetheless, at a press conference on January 18, he credited much of his forces' initial success to information gathered during the preceding months, not only photint but elint and comint as well. "As in the early days of any battle," stated Schwarzkopf, "the fog of war is present, but having been in the outset of several battles myself, I would tell you that we probably have a more accurate picture of what's going on in Operation Desert Storm than I have ever had before in the early hours of battle."

Processing all the data posed its own considerable problems. Pho-

to interpreters, for example, had little breathing space. U.S. satellites almost continuously transmitted data that had to be sifted, scrutinized, and distributed. The deluge of information was overwhelming. Peter Zimmerman, reconnaissance expert and professor at George Washington University, provided an apt analogy: "If you've ever tried to drink water from a fire hose, you understand how much information our image interpreters can get hit with every day." Former Air Force Secretary Edward Aldridge takes the problem a step further when dealing with tactical needs. "Somewhere in that data is a target," he said. "Now, how do you find it—unless you take the population of the United States and make them photo interpreters?" Efforts to automate the profession through the use of supercomputers to filter and interpret data have helped, but as Aldridge explained, "we're still years away from the point where some data comes in and rings a bell and says, 'I've got a target X on location Y.' "

With the military rivalry between the United States and the Soviet Union in recession, it might seem that the demand for photo-

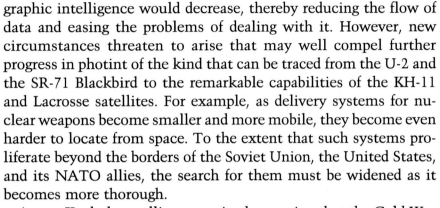

graphic intelligence would decrease, thereby reducing the flow of data and easing the problems of dealing with it. However, new circumstances threaten to arise that may well compel further progress in photint of the kind that can be traced from the U-2 and the SR-71 Blackbird to the remarkable capabilities of the KH-11 and Lacrosse satellites. For example, as delivery systems for nuclear weapons become smaller and more mobile, they become even harder to locate from space. To the extent that such systems proliferate beyond the borders of the Soviet Union, the United States, and its NATO allies, the search for them must be widened as it becomes more thorough.

A new Keyhole satellite, conceived assuming that the Cold War would continue indefinitely but diligently pursued as the new world order unfolds, is in the works. Some who follow this technology from outside the secret warrens of the intelligence community predict that it will have an on-board system to alert ground controllers of imminent attack by antisatellite weapons. Already there are satellites in orbit that can detect the extremely hot exhaust from the launch of even a small ballistic missile, such as the Scuds launched by Iraq against Israel and Saudi Arabia during the Gulf War. The overhead vantage point might be ideal for tracking the flight of stealth aircraft that are difficult to see with ground-based radar. In addition to new TDRSS satellites capable of transmitting data at a much faster rate than current models, there will be new radar satellites, deploying antennas perhaps 300 feet across, to tax their capacities. From orbits up to 1,000 miles above earth, they will be able to provide imagery of higher resolution than even Lacrosse can muster.

The bill for these projects would be enormous. It has been estimated that to construct and launch the generation of satellites already on the drawing boards, keep the TR-1 spyplanes in operation, man the ground stations, and handle the massive amounts of data would cost more than $50 billion per year. But because of new arms-control agreements that require constant surveillance, and the prospect of other nations acquiring the ability to build nuclear or chemical weapons, there seems to be no alternative to pressing forward. Photint will remain an important means of following the axiom: Know thine enemy. ★

Computer Tricks for
the Interpreter's Trade

The pictures obtained by satellites and spyplanes are raw material that must be processed by expert interpreters to yield useful intelligence. A casual observer studying this busy aerial view of naval facilities at Norfolk, Virginia, would be hard-pressed to extract such prime details as the whereabouts of two ships with helicopter landing pads. (Xs mark the spots.) In some cases, even after experts have analyzed an image and pinpointed a strategic feature, untrained eyes may find it unrecognizable. When CIA photo interpreters showed President John Kennedy and his aides U-2 shots of a nuclear missile base under construction in Cuba, the president was baffled. One aide marveled that the evidence consisted of "barely discernible scratches."

At the time, the photo interpreters who made sense of such scratches had to rely mainly on keen vision, a good memory, and a few basic enhancement techniques, notably magnification. But now, the computer is beginning to transform the art of interpretation. By reducing an image to thousands of tiny points, or pixels, and assigning each pixel a number based on its brightness, computers can manipulate the image on command. An interpreter can select one area of interest on the computer screen, for example, and heighten its contrast. If that stratagem proves fruitless, the original pixel values can be recalled from the computer's memory in seconds, and the operator can try another approach. In wartime, this quick digital maneuvering not only helps target identification and post-strike damage assessment but speeds the task of transforming aerial views of enemy territory into accurate maps and other aids to success.

For all the high-tech wizardry, the interpreter's most important asset remains the human power of recognition—the talent for spotting a familiar face in a seemingly unvaried throng. Until machines can discriminate with equal finesse, individuals must make the subtle distinctions on which interpretation depends.

A true-color satellite image of a Soviet military facility *(above, left)* offers an indistinct view of an innocuous dark dot *(center, bottom)* surrounded by a circular gray area. Digital enhancement to heighten the contrast in the gray area *(above, right)* reveals the distinctive six-point layout of a surface-to-air missile battery.

Bringing Out Hidden Details

Pictures relayed from satellites orbiting hundreds of miles above the earth are seldom clear enough to tell photo interpreters everything that they need to know. Haze in the atmosphere, shadows cast by clouds, or the inherent limitations of the satellite's sensors may leave important areas ill defined. Once an interpreter has identified such zones, however, the computer can be used to enhance them in various ways. One technique, shown above, involves redistributing pixel values so that subtle differences in brightness are accentuated; overall, the image loses a degree of clarity, but significant details emerge in the area of interest.

To identify camouflaged objects, interpreters may have to look beyond the visible range—an approach made possible by the use of multispectral sensors on satellites. It is not unusual for reconnaissance orbiters to collect light in both the visible and the infrared (IR) bands of the spectrum. Sensors for the long-wave portion of the infrared band detect heat. Those tuned to shorter-wave segments are sensitive to energy reflected by chlorophyll and thus can be used to distinguish between vegetation and man-made objects *(right)*.

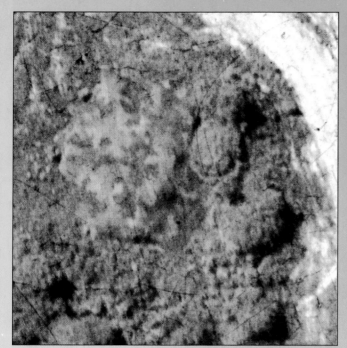 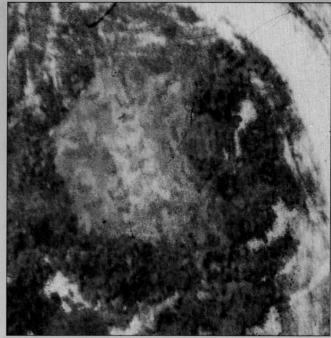

To unmask hidden weaponry, interpreters work with shorter-wave infrared data. The IR image above shows vegetation with a mottled area in its midst that suggests camouflage and calls for further analysis. An enhanced version of the image *(above, right)* heightens the infrared contrast between the camouflage netting and the live vegetation around it. A similar enhancement, combined with the first, produces the image at right. Color added by computer accentuates areas that reflect most brightly, including a rectangular object, probably made of metal, under the netting. Though indistinct, the shape has the look of a vehicle—possibly a tank.

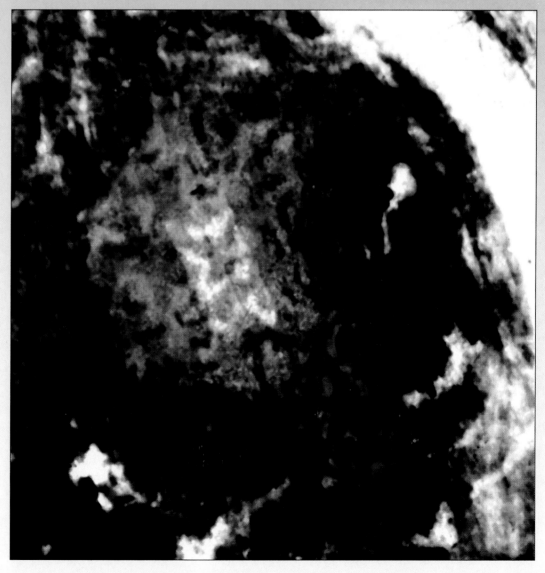

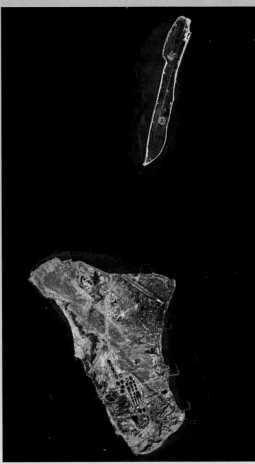

Satellite views show Kharg Island in the Persian Gulf—site of an Iranian oil-storage facility—and a smaller island to its north as they appeared in 1986 *(far left)* and 1987 *(left)*. To bring out changes there during the year, a period of warfare between Iran and Iraq, interpreters projected the images in different colors and fused them *(right)* so that features unique to the 1986 view would appear dark blue and the 1987 additions would appear orange. The fusion reveals some minor changes. One ship lies at the dock *(far right)* in 1987 compared with two in 1986. Other blue- and orange-colored patches suggest shifts in the levels of ponds and storage tanks. But one development stands out: The orange circle on the small island represents an air-defense site—perhaps antiaircraft artillery—newly installed by the Iraqis.

Keeping Track of Developments

Image interpreters look for change—more activity this week than last, an object missing today from a position it occupied yesterday. Such developments can be the first sure sign of an adversary's intentions. Yet meaningful changes in successive images can be so subtle as to elude notice by the most skilled of observers.

Digital processing makes change detection less taxing and more certain by bringing sequential images together in revealing ways. One computer technique involves flashing two successive images alternately onto the screen so that changes seem to jump out at the viewer. Another method, illustrated here, relies on the simple expe-dient of processing the two images in contrasting colors before combining them so that the common features blend together into one shade while the changes take on a different tint.

These methods are extremely helpful in cases where only slight alteration has occurred. When an area has undergone a thorough transformation, however, the computer may overwhelm interpreters with cues, making the important developments hard to distinguish from the trivial. Programmers are now trying to equip computers with some degree of discrimination, so that they can recognize important changes and bring them to the interpreter's attention.

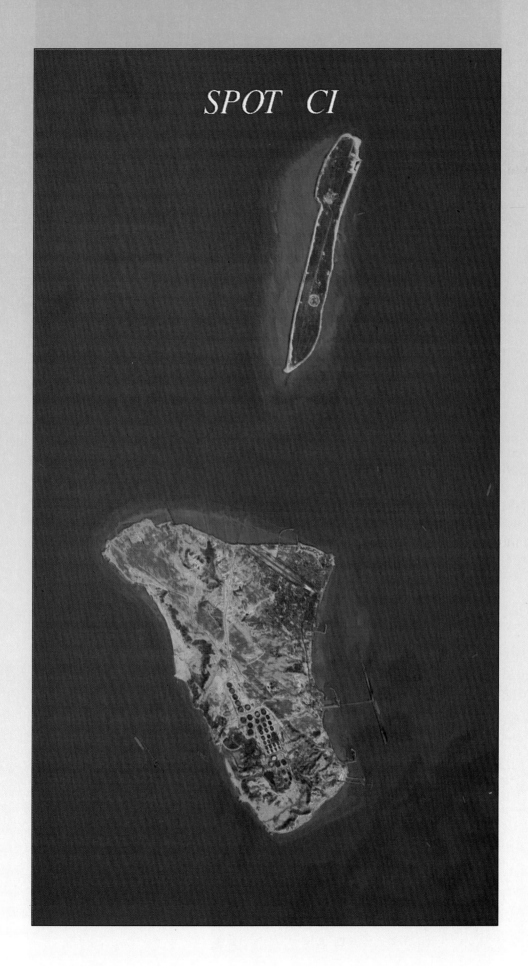

SPOT CI

High-altitude views such as the satellite image of a German town at near right provide the standard against which an image interpreter measures the accuracy of an existing map of the same area *(middle)* and makes revisions. In this case, when the satellite view is superimposed on a printed map that has been scanned into a computer, the combined image *(far right)* reveals a serious discrepancy. As shown in the circular closeup, the roads marked on the map do not correspond to the routes photographed by the satellite *(traced in* white*)*—a problem that stems from a small mapmaking error. Discarding the entire map and preparing a new one from scratch would be prohibitively expensive and time-consuming. Instead, the programmer instructs the computer to adjust the map until the roads are aligned with the satellite view *(lower right).* This quick fix will yield a revised map with dependable coordinates that can be printed and supplied to an artillery crew, for example, for targeting a discrete point such as a road junction.

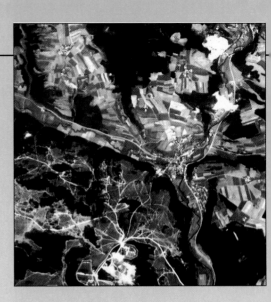

Artful Assists for Commanders

In wartime, image interpreters provide tactical aid to mission planners by converting the latest aerial views of enemy territory into maps and charts that tell attackers exactly where the target is and what obstacles stand in the way. The conversion process involves new applications of old techniques such as stereo imagery—two shots of the same target, taken from slightly different angles, that form a three-dimensional image when viewed together. Using relief information gleaned from stereo images, computers can quickly produce such tools as the line-of-sight chart below, which lets troops know where terrain will conceal them from the enemy. Above all, computers have enhanced tactical image processing by expediting it. During World War II, producing an updated map based on aerial photographs could take days, during which bombing, floods, or enemy activity might alter the landscape. Today, within hours of the time a satellite passes over a target area and relays its data, an interpreter can generate a computerized map that is more precise than its handmade predecessor.

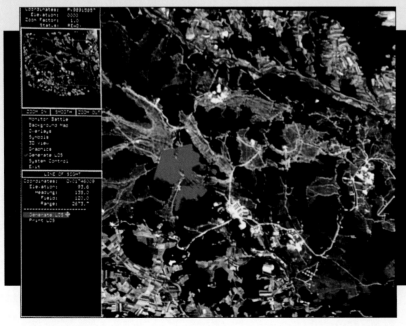

SEEING WHAT CAN BE SEEN

Generated by a computer from stereo images obtained by satellite, this line-of-sight projection highlights in red the field of view for a human observer or a radar antenna looking southeast from the top of a hill. The computer program can furnish this information for any point on the map that an attacker might choose to assault or a defender might want to hold.

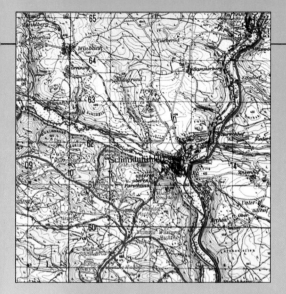
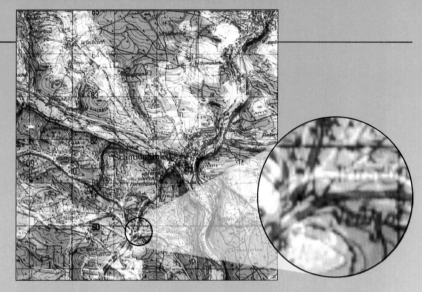
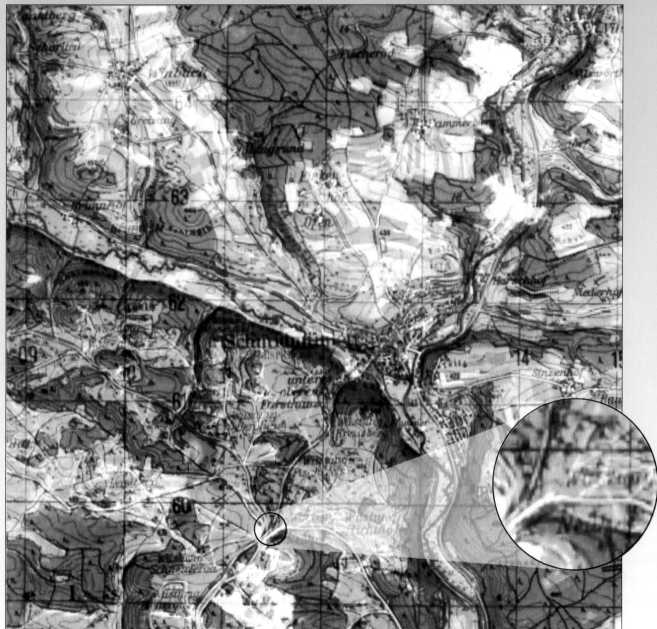

To produce the perspective view of a
mountain peak at right, technicians first
instructed a computer to combine the satellite picture above with a digitized topo-
graphical map of the area, assigning each
pixel of the photograph a height taken
from the map. Supplied with such information, the computer can be instructed
to show the scene from any point of view
simply by repositioning the red pointer.

Improving the Prospects for Attackers

Perhaps the neatest optical trick interpreters can perform for military planners is the conversion of overhead shots into oblique views that show what pilots will see from the cockpit, for example, when they streak in toward a target at low level.

Older methods of bringing high-altitude images down to earth involved slowly gauging the relative height of the various features by examining stereo images or by measuring the lengths of shadows in a conventional photograph. The results would then be translated into side-view drawings or three-dimensional models.

Creating a model as detailed as the computer images shown below might take six specialists up to 2,000 hours—long enough for conditions in the target area to change dramatically. With computers crunching the digits from stereo images, interpreters need supply only height information to generate a lifelike perspective view.

More important, the program can quickly accommodate changes in a mission. If planners decide at the last minute to shift the axis of attack to avoid strengthened air defenses, for example, the computer can promptly provide a view of the new route.

Of Wavelengths and Pulse Rates

During a test in the California desert, a U.S. Navy AGM-88 high-speed, antiradiation missile (HARM) explodes directly above a radar antenna. Once electronic intelligence (elint) has identified the frequencies used by enemy radar, anti-radiation missiles such as the aircraft-launched HARM can be programmed to seek out the radar's pulses and follow them to their source, to destroy the enemy's electronic eyes.

On August 31, 1983, the fifteen crew members of an RC-135S Cobra Ball electronic-reconnaissance plane slipped into their olive drab flight suits, boarded the big jet with the profile of a Boeing 707, and prepared for takeoff along a dark runway at Shemya in the Aleutian Islands. Bathed in the eerie green glow from their monitors, the U.S. Air Force specialists concentrated on their duties as the mission began and remained unperturbed by the fact that their assignment would carry them along the coast of Siberia within easy range of Soviet interceptors. The prime objective of the Cobra Ball flight was to record radio signals emanating from a Soviet ballistic missile during an anticipated test flight; the signals, called telemetry, would tell the missile controllers—and the Americans monitoring their efforts—how the missile was performing by detailing its attitude, thrust, and fuel-consumption rate. The crew of the RC-135S also planned to use special cameras to film the fiery reentry of the missile's warhead. Along the way, they would listen for Soviet radar signals originating on the Kamchatka Peninsula, a 750-mile-long landmass jutting out between the Bering Sea and the Sea of Okhotsk.

The Kamchatka Peninsula and nearby Sakhalin Island were dotted with military bases guarded by a network of air-defense installations. Early-warning radars swept large sectors of the sky with fan-shaped beams to detect incoming planes up to 200 miles away. Tracking radars, situated near batteries of surface-to-air missiles, used narrower, shorter-range beams to pinpoint potential threats for the jets that would challenge any intruder. Backing them up were fire-control radars that, after locking onto the target with a pencil-thin beam, would guide surface-to-air missiles to the mark.

Although the flight path of the RC-135S would bring the aircraft within the coverage of early-warning and tracking radars, the pilot had been ordered to remain at least forty miles outside the borders of the Soviet Union to preclude any hostile response. On previous occasions, however, other surveillance planes dedicated to collecting data on Soviet air defenses had edged much closer to shore to draw fire-control radars into play as well; on-board instruments had then pinpointed the various sites and recorded the signals to assist in the development of countermeasures for U.S. warplanes should they ever be called on to penetrate those defenses in earnest.

The Cobra Ball flight of August 31 proceeded without incident. As it turned out, no missile was launched that night. Five hours into the flight, the pilot of the RC-135S curved eastward, safely skirting the tip of the Kamchatka Peninsula and looping back toward his base in the Aleutians.

But all was not quiet on the invisible electronic front separating the superpowers. As the RC-135S turned away from Kamchatka around 1:00 a.m., another plane was approaching Soviet air space there—Korean Air Lines Flight 007, a Boeing 747 en route from Anchorage, Alaska, to Seoul with 269 people aboard. The distinctive jumbo jet, nearly half again as long as an RC-135, was 400 miles off course, probably because its inertial navigation system had been misprogrammed at the start of the flight. This gaping error brought Flight 007 within range of the radar sites that had been tracking the RC-135, a coincidence that may have led the Soviets to suspect that it was the same plane looping back toward their territory. In any case, when the airliner headed across the southern tip of Kamchatka, four interceptors were dispatched from the base at Petropavlovsk. The jets failed to spot their quarry before it cleared Kamchatka and reentered international air space over the Sea of Okhotsk. But even greater danger lay ahead for Flight 007. Ignorant of his plight, the pilot was heading straight for strategic Sakhalin Island, and the Soviets there were now on full alert.

As the jetliner cruised nearer, a call went out to the Sokol air base ordering Lieutenant Colonel Gennadiy Osipovich to enter the cockpit of his Su-15 interceptor, a twin-engine jet with a top speed of 1,500 miles per hour, and be ready to take off at a moment's notice. Osipovich, who had flown patrols in the Far East for ten years, had returned two weeks earlier from a leave taken at the insistence of his regimental doctor following months of tension at the base. According to the pilot, that April a U.S. plane had trespassed on Soviet air space along the fog-shrouded coast for fifteen minutes without being intercepted. A military commission had reprimanded Osipovich and his fellow pilots for the failure. Nerves had begun to fray, and Osipovich had welcomed the time away from base. But April was still fresh in his memory as he settled into the seat of his fighter a few hours before dawn on September 1.

When tracking radar indicated that the intruder was about to reenter Soviet air space off Sakhalin, Osipovich was ordered aloft to join five other interceptors in the chase. Ground controllers guided Osipovich in an approach to Flight 007 from behind. He first caught sight of the plane through a thin layer of cloud from a distance of more than seven miles. He could not identify his quarry, but he informed his controller that its red and green navigation lights were blinking. Asked later what he was thinking at the moment, Osipovich replied that he was conscious only of a sharp excitement. He likened his role to that of a watchdog trained to distinguish the strange from the familiar. All he knew at the time was that what lay ahead was "something strange."

Keeping his distance from the intruder, Osipovich reported that he had locked onto the target with his aircraft's radar. A short time later, Osipovich recounted, the controller announced that the target had violated Soviet air space and ordered it destroyed, only to rescind the command within seconds: "Abort destruction! Match altitude with the target and force it to land."

Osipovich closed to within a few miles of the aircraft, but he lacked tracer rounds for his cannon that would have attracted the intruder's attention. At the ground controller's insistence, he fired some cannon bursts anyway, to no effect. Osipovich thought that he might make an impression by flashing at the aircraft with his landing lights, and after he did so it appeared to reduce its speed. He could see now that it was a very large plane, one that resembled no foreign military or reconnaissance aircraft he knew of. But time had run out for Flight 007. The airliner was barely ninety seconds from safety in international air space. Determined that the intruder must not escape, whatever its identity or intent, the controller reinstated his original order: "Destroy the target!"

Osipovich fired two missiles, one guided by radar and the other by the heat of the target's engines. "I have executed the launch," he reported calmly. One missile, most likely the heat seeker, severed the plane's left wing; the other punched a large hole in the tail section of the jumbo jet. Tumbling out of control, the crippled 747 plunged into the sea with a crushing impact that left no survivors.

The destruction of the plane and its passengers shocked the

world, but Soviet officials showed no remorse. When pressed for an explanation, they claimed that the 747 was a spyplane following a prescribed route over sensitive military installations; to back up their story, they fabricated details to make it appear that the jumbo jet was operating in tandem with the RC-135 and that the airliner's pilot had ignored clear warnings. Osipovich, who considered the controller's order to shoot consistent with Soviet policy, was annoyed when his superiors refused to speak frankly and defend their longstanding practice of dealing aggressively with intruders. "They began to lie about the small things," he confided years later to a Russian journalist investigating the incident. "They said that the aircraft was flying without lights or flashers, that tracer rounds were used to fire warning shots, that I talked to it on the radio."

As international pressure mounted on the Soviets to justify their actions, propagandists presented Osipovich with a "libretto," a doctored account for the pilot to recite on television. He complied, but his performance lacked spontaneity. So Osipovich asked the pro-

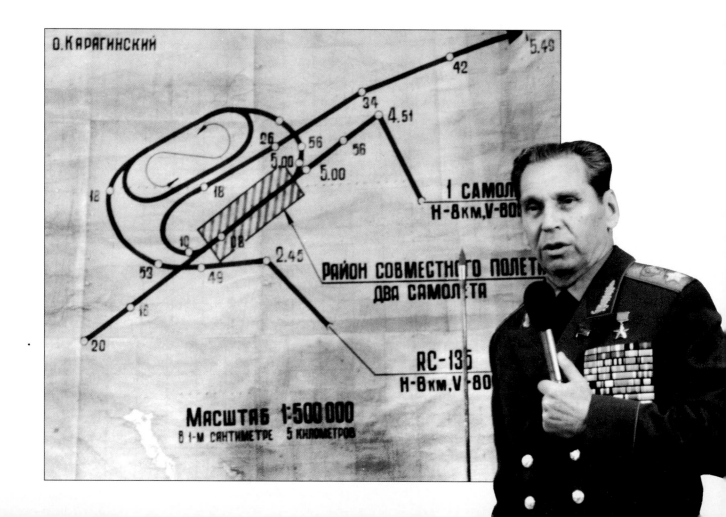

ducer for a break, drank a bottle of vodka, and tried again, departing from the prepared text to ramble on about the lessons to be drawn from the incident and the dangers of nuclear war.

Moscow's clumsy attempt to distort the record proved futile, in part because U.S. listening posts in Japan had recorded the radio transmissions of Osipovich and another pilot who had shadowed Flight 007 during its last minutes. The tapes, played before the United Nations Security Council, punctured the claims made by the Soviets and left many listeners astonished by their willingness to shoot down the plane without first establishing hostile intent.

But the deadly incident came as less of a surprise to those familiar with the turbulent history of electronic spying during the Cold War. The twin branches of intelligence gathering known as elint and telint—aimed at radar and telemetry respectively—were so important to the military preparedness of the superpowers that for decades they had haunted each other's borders to gain an edge in the event of war. With the help of a superior air-defense system, American pilots had consistently managed to escort potential Soviet intruders away from U.S. air space without having to open fire. Frustrated by such vigilance, the Soviets may have installed surveillance devices on civilian Aeroflot aircraft bound to and from Washington, D.C.; more than once, those flights had departed inexplicably from their assigned paths and overflown U.S. bases. In the meantime, repeated feints and isolated incursions by U.S. ferret planes, as the electronic snoopers were known, had left Soviet defenders in a state of wariness bordering on paranoia.

This dangerous game had its roots in World War II, when the fledgling science of radar grew swiftly to maturity. Early on, the British demonstrated the power of the new tool by using it to read the German blitz and avert conquest, and thereafter the warring powers made the detection of enemy radar emissions a top priority. With the help of such elint, engineers developed jamming devices and other electronic countermeasures (ECM) to thwart radar. Antidotes to radar were crafted in the laboratory, but much of the intelligence that made them possible was culled by spyplanes operating near or in enemy air space. When the hot war between the Allies and the Axis gave way to a cold one between East and West, ferret flights remained essential because new weapons systems developed by both sides depended for guidance on radar that was constantly upgraded to frustrate existing ECM. Only superior coun-

At a Moscow press conference, Marshal Nikolai Ogarkov offers the Soviet version of the events that led to the 1983 downing of Korean Air Lines Flight 007. The box on the chart shows where, according to Ogarkov, the path of the airliner (straight line) paralleled that of a U.S.A.F. RC-135 Cobra Ball aircraft for ten minutes. Citing these fabricated plots, the Soviets charged that the planes had been spying in concert; in actuality, the American aircraft had already landed in the Aleutian Islands at the times posted on this map.

termeasures, derived from keener surveillance tools, could offer an attacker a good chance of penetrating the enemy's electronic web.

Along with improved elint sensors came new platforms, or collection vehicles, for obtaining the vital information. Starting in the 1960s, ferret planes and receivers based on land or at sea were supplemented by computerized drones that could circle over radar installations and high-flying satellites that could snare faint signals from strategic missiles more than 20,000 miles below. Except when disasters such as the downing of Flight 007 occurred, few other than intelligence specialists even heard about such activities in peacetime or fathomed the importance of the emissions that the various intelligence platforms monitored. When a shooting war loomed, however, as it did in the Persian Gulf after the Iraqi invasion of Kuwait in 1990, the seemingly arcane business of electronic snooping took on an urgency that every pilot, soldier, or civilian endangered by an Iraqi SAM or Scud could appreciate. And to the top commanders, elint represented more than a hedge against particular weapons systems: It offered a formula for the wholesale suppression of enemy air defenses.

First Moves in an Electronic Chess Match

On August 2, 1939, one month before war erupted in Europe, the giant airship *Graf Zeppelin* lifted off from a field in northern Germany and glided across the English Channel in the dark to perform the world's first ferret flight. The mission was prompted by German intelligence reports that the English had erected a series of antennas up to 300 feet high along the coast from Southampton to Newcastle. Nazi agents there had described them as broadcasting towers. But some officials in Berlin feared that the antennas might represent a major breakthrough in military technology.

German researchers had been working on an air-defense system that would use antennas to bounce ultrahigh-frequency radio waves off incoming enemy planes, thus fixing their location. The process was simple enough in theory. Since radio signals, like all electromagnetic waves, move at the speed of light, the distance of an incoming plane from the antenna could be computed by measuring the time it took for an impulse to reach the intruder and return to the emitter. Known as radio detecting and ranging—or radar, for short—the technique posed major problems for engineers. For one thing, measurement of the signal's travel time had to be extremely precise, since an error of a thousandth of a second would skew the distance calculation by more than ninety miles. For another, the various radar sites had to be linked up electronically to provide air-defense coordinators with a coherent picture of the enemy threat. Germany had yet to devise such a network when reports reached Berlin of the large antennas along the English coast.

To check out the disturbing possibility that the British had beaten them to the punch, the Germans outfitted the *Graf Zeppelin* with antennas and other electronic gear designed to intercept and record emissions from the towers as the airship slipped silently along the coast. Through the night, teams of specialists under the watchful eye of General Wolfgang Martini, head of the Luftwaffe's Signal Corps, adjusted their equipment in a vain attempt to pick up revealing signals. When the crew returned to Germany with nothing to show for their efforts, skeptics who had contended that British radar posed no threat were strengthened in their delusion by the inconclusive results. Luftwaffe chief Hermann Göring, for one, felt confident that his air force was unstoppable and dismissed the entire issue of electronic defenses as peripheral.

Just why the *Graf Zeppelin* failed to detect signals from the British radar antennas has not been established. Perhaps the receivers hastily installed on the airship malfunctioned or were scanning the wrong frequencies. Although the portion of the electromagnetic spectrum then used for radar transmissions was narrow compared to that exploited later, it was still broad enough to confound spies who had no idea where to look for a signal within the band. Or perhaps the British turned off their sets to forestall detection. In any case, the fruitless mission left the Germans ill-prepared for the British response when the Luftwaffe launched a full-scale air assault a year later. Royal Air Force fighter pilots, guided by radar toward incoming German bombers and their escorts, converged swiftly on the pressure points rather than aimlessly patrolling huge volumes of empty sky. The guidance enabled the RAF to make the most of its dwindling assets and thwart the larger Luftwaffe.

Aside from leading the way in radar technology, the British made the first systematic efforts to gather elint. Conventional intelligence methods, including the interrogation of captured pilots, revealed early on that the Germans were not only refining defensive radar but applying techniques for guiding bombers toward targets at night or in poor weather using lower-frequency radio transmissions. RAF reconnaissance pilots began to listen through their headphones for suspicious signals, and in late June of 1940 one of them hit pay dirt, picking up a series of Morse code dots, followed by a continuous tone, then a series of dashes. It turned out that the signals were emanating from two German antennas situated side by side so that their beams overlapped, one transmitting dots and the other dashes. A Luftwaffe bomber flying the prescribed path toward England would remain within the intersection of the two beams and hear a continuous signal through his headphones; dots or dashes signaled the need for a course correction.

Once elint had identified the frequency at which the twin antennas were transmitting, the British had to choose between two basic ECM options, one involving brute force and the other sleight of hand. The first possibility was to overwhelm the dots and dashes by emitting a more powerful continuous signal at the same frequency. Such jamming would foil the guidance system but would also alert the Germans to the fact that the system had been exposed. So the British resorted instead to a more subtle tactic, transmitting the same pattern of dots and dashes from radio towers in England so that the signals led the German bombers to open fields. These the British disguised as significant targets by installing powerful searchlights there and setting huge fires as the bombs hit.

Buoyed by the results, the British extended their electronic surveillance to cover the emerging German radar network. A fierce technological duel ensued, in which successful countermeasures spawned by elint were analyzed by the enemy and foiled with counter-countermeasures (ECCM) that demanded an even more sophisticated response. By monitoring the first German early-warning radars, for example, the British found that all the sites operated at the same frequency and tailored a jamming device to overwhelm it. In response, the Germans devised a more versatile radar that could be tuned to transmit at different frequencies on different occasions. Eventually, the British cracked that system as well and introduced an adaptable jammer that could match the German emissions wavelength for wavelength.

In July 1943, the British scored another first on the electronic front when their bombers initiated the use of chaff—strips of metallic foil cut to measure roughly half the wavelength of enemy

Lieutenant Jacob Beser, electronic officer on the two flights that dropped atomic bombs on Japan in 1945, stands before the *Enola Gay*, the B-29 flown on the first nuclear mission. In a pioneering elint effort, Beser selected and operated the equipment used to monitor Japanese radar signals, which could have inadvertently set off the radar proximity fuzes used to detonate the atomic bomb at a precise, predetermined altitude.

radar frequencies as determined through elint. Released at high altitude, the clouds of reflective strips covered German radar screens with bright splotches that made it hard for the ground controllers to discern the real threats. Soon bombers on both sides were deploying chaff. Since the radar sites defending any given target area might employ a range of frequencies, strips of different lengths were cut before a mission and dispensed in mixed bundles over the area. Included among the crew members on some flights was an electronic-warfare specialist, equipped with a radar receiver and headphones, who timed the release of chaff bundles, set jamming devices to the appropriate wavelength, and gathered elint for future missions. American B-29s flying long bombing runs against the Japanese in the Pacific carried the specialist and his gear crammed in between the bulkhead and the chemical toilet, whose seat provided the only perch for the Raven, as such electronic officers were known.

Elint played a significant if unheralded role in the momentous flight of the *Enola Gay*, the B-29 that delivered an atomic bomb over the city of Hiroshima on August 6, 1945. Mission planners had calculated that for maximum effect, the bomb should detonate at a height of 1,900 feet. One fuze available for the purpose gauged altitude through changes in barometric pressure, but the system's margin of error was considerable. Far more accurate was a radar proximity fuze that measured height above the ground by timing the echo of a signal beamed to earth. This type of detonator, however, posed a risk. If the Japanese happened to be transmitting signals at the same frequency as the radar ranging device—or even at a precise fraction or multiple of that frequency—then the bomb could detonate prematurely, dissipating the force of the explosion and possibly destroying the B-29. A decision was made to rely on radar fuzing but to equip the bomb with a backup barometric fuze as well and switch to it if enemy signals at a dangerous frequency were detected near the target.

The task of monitoring enemy transmissions aboard the *Enola Gay* fell to Lieutenant Jacob Beser, the electronic officer of the B-29 squadron assigned to carry out the crucial mission. As the plane approached Hiroshima, Beser listened intently through the head-phones of his APR-4 receiver, a wide-spectrum device that covered all the frequencies that might affect the radar fuzes. Detecting no signals at those settings, Beser adhered to the plan for radar deto-nation. The bomb exploded at the prescribed altitude, with a ter-rible impact that brought the Japanese government to the verge of surrender. Three days later, Beser was the only member of the *Enola Gay* crew to fly the second atomic mission, against Nagasaki. Once again, the frequencies he monitored were clear of interfering sig-nals; the bomb detonated at the optimum height, obliterating Na-gasaki and with it the last vestiges of enemy resistance.

Lessons learned on the electronic front in the heat of battle during World War II were not forgotten by the opposing camps in the cold war that followed. Escalating tensions between the United States and the USSR led to the development of sharper elint tools. In the late 1940s, for example, a team of American engineers at the Naval Research Laboratory came up with a way to retrieve Soviet radar signals that eluded ocean- or land-based receivers situated over the horizon from the transmitter. Such signals followed a straight line into space, seemingly lost forever. Some of them, however, struck the moon, which reflected the signals toward earth. To capture them, engineers designed a giant bowl-shaped antenna of great sen-sitivity. At first Project Moonbounce, as the endeavor was known, yielded little because the moon was in the proper position to reflect signals to the fixed antenna only about forty minutes each day. To solve that problem, the team perfected a dish that could pivot to follow the moon's course. In addition to receiving signals, the in-strument could be used to compute the angle at which the signals struck the moon, fixing the radar's position within five miles.

Such safe long-distance spying helped flesh out the portrait of Russian radar techniques, but the main details were filled in by ferret planes that began prowling the Soviet borders soon after World War II ended. The first such aircraft adapted for service along the Siberian coast, a B-29, had its gun turrets removed and carried radar receivers in place of bombs. After modification, the recon-naissance plane was known officially as an RB-29, but the crew members, realizing that they would be helpless if Russian inter-ceptors contested their presence, dubbed it the *Sitting Duck*. Once, a shift in the jet stream deflected the high-flying propeller-driven aircraft from its intended route off the coast and carried it fifty miles inland. "Why don't we get the hell out of here?" shouted one of the Ravens to the navigator, who explained that the aircraft was trying to do just that but laboring against the fierce headwind at a mere "twenty knots ground speed." The *Sitting Duck* appeared to be living up to its name. Fortunately for the intruders, Soviet defenses along the coast proved less than competent, permitting the plane to complete its agonizingly slow retreat unchallenged.

Altogether, the first RB-29 completed eight missions along the Siberian coast without being intercepted, a record that underscored the deficiencies of the Soviet air-defense system. At the time, few of the 20,000 Russian combat aircraft carried radar, and coordination between ground controllers and interceptors was poor. Goaded by the ferret flights, however, the Soviets made significant strides within a few years. Harvesting elint became an increasingly dangerous business, not only for the men aboard the modest-paced RB-29s but also for the crews of swifter, jet-powered reconnaissance aircraft such as the RB-47, which carried limited defensive armament. By 1960, more than a dozen American ferret planes had been shot from the skies or otherwise forced down by the Soviets.

Such flights persisted despite the risks because they were providing vital data on advances in Russian radar technology. Both the United States and the USSR were introducing so-called agile radars that could hop from frequency to frequency and vary their pulse-repetition rates. U.S. spyplanes could tell that these antics were being performed by one radar station rather than many because the aircraft carried electronic direction finders that indicated where an impulse was coming from regardless of its permutations. Countering the versatile systems was another matter, however. Conventional jamming devices had to be set in advance to anticipate the radar's characteristics, and frequency-agile radar was hard to predict. In response, the U.S. Air Force came up with a device that automatically scanned the range across which Soviet radars were known to skip and jammed the signals as soon as it detected them. The so-called sweep jammer had its limits. In the fraction of a second it took to catch up with a frequency change, an alert radar operator might pick up an accurate return from the intruder. In addition, the band width that the device could cover was limited by the size of the antenna a warplane could carry.

In time, airborne sweep jammers would become faster and more agile. But ground radar stations would always be able to apply more power and deploy larger antennas. As a result, the United States strived in the early 1960s to perfect a potent ECM alternative— missiles that could home on radar emitters. Ferret flights set the stage for such strikes not only by tracking radar sites but by fingerprinting them, a process that involved displaying the wave energy on an oscilloscope and recording the results on film. Analysis of the fingerprint revealed certain characteristics that remained constant regardless of changes in frequency or pulse-repetition rate. That data was used to craft electronic sensors capable of distinguishing the emissions of a particular enemy radar system from other signals in the environment. Alerted by the sensors, crewmen on U.S. warplanes could then target the sites with missiles that rode the emissions back to their source.

The increasing complexity of elint tasks—and the desire of intelligence officers to gather telint from the same platforms—led to a demand for a larger ferret plane that could house heavy antennas

and bulky computers for data storage. The RB-47, an aircraft with less capacity than the RB-29, was not the answer. For a time, the Air Force went forward with production of an armed reconnaissance version of its big strategic bomber, the B-52. But events in 1960 led to a reassessment of that program. In May, after a U-2 spyplane piloted by Gary Powers was shot down over the Soviet Union, President Dwight Eisenhower declared an end to U.S. overflights of Soviet territory; the ban applied to elint missions as well as photint, although on rare occasions U.S. ferret planes would still stray briefly across the twelve-mile limit into Soviet air space. Then, on July 1, an RB-47 was downed by Soviet interceptors in international air space over the Barents Sea. Four of the six crewmen perished; Soviet vessels picked up the other two and delivered them to captivity. The United States protested the action and obtained the release of the two captives after seven months. But the Soviets reserved the right to challenge any U.S. aircraft configured like a bomber.

In fact, there was little to be gained by provoking the Soviets along their borders. A ferret plane carrying the latest equipment could compile an exhaustive dossier on Soviet radar defenses while remaining beyond the twelve-mile limit. Accordingly, the Air Force dropped the RB-52 program and introduced a roomy new reconnaissance aircraft built along the lines of a Boeing 707 jetliner. Designated the RC-135, the unarmed aircraft, whose ten-hour endurance could be extended by in-flight refueling, became the mainstay of U.S. elint efforts for the next three decades.

On a typical ferret flight, the jet would carry a crew of up to twenty-one along with ten tons of gear. Ravens used to marathon

An Air Force RC-135S bristles with antennas and sensor pods for monitoring Soviet ballistic missile tests. As an economy measure, this plane carries its electronic sensors and cameras on the right side of the fuselage only. The antennas primarily responsible for gathering missile telemetry reside in the nose and in the ridges on the fuselage, just forward of the wing.

missions in cramped quarters were delighted to have a chance to stretch out in flight. On longer sorties, the men worked in two shifts, with those off-duty retiring to a rest area replete with bunks. Each specialist had his own console; several recorded enemy transmissions, while others eavesdropped on verbal communications, sometimes learning that an interceptor had been sent to confront them. RC-135s did not come under direct attack by the Soviets, but the pilots experienced other forms of intimidation from interceptors—including the practice known as thumping, in which a MiG would sneak up behind the ferret and rock the plane with a blast from its afterburner as it streaked by less than twenty feet away.

The Soviets increased their own elint capability in the mid-1960s when they introduced a big spyplane to rival the RC-135. Designated the TU-95 Bear, this converted bomber was powered by four turboprop engines and boasted a range of 10,000 miles and a top speed of 500 miles an hour. A typical ferret mission carried a Bear from its base on the Kola Peninsula, bordering the Barents Sea, all the way to Cuba on a trajectory that paralleled the east coast of the United States. American radar operators monitored the flights closely, and any Bear that ventured within a few miles of U.S. air space was sure to be met by interceptors and escorted off.

A Fateful Foray into the Tonkin Gulf

Aside from their hazardous Cold War duties, ferret planes collected tactical intelligence in times of open conflict. RC-135s amassed elint over Vietnam in the 1960s and later off the coast of Libya and in the Persian Gulf. But not everything military commanders needed to know about enemy radar and ECM could be garnered from platforms in the air. From its inception, radar was a prime concern of naval intelligence as well. Just as ferret planes prowled the skies, warships bristling with antennas stood vigil at sea, scanning enemy frequencies. Maritime ferreting could be every bit as risky as its aerial counterpart. Indeed, it was a contested elint mission by an American vessel in the Tonkin Gulf that led to the congressional resolution committing the United States to the war in Vietnam.

On July 31, 1964, the destroyer *Maddox* entered the Tonkin Gulf to scout the North Vietnamese coast. Built in 1944, the *Maddox* had recently been equipped with the latest in electronic surveillance

gear, including an automatic pulse analyzer that recorded radar waves on film. The mission came at a time when U.S.-aided South Vietnamese forces were trying to infiltrate spies and commandos along the coast as part of their ongoing war with the Communists. Only the night before, the South Vietnamese had attempted unsuccessfully to land commandos on two North Vietnamese islands in the gulf. In the aftermath, the North Vietnamese were on the lookout, transforming what one briefing officer had described as a "Sunday cruise" for the *Maddox* into a tightrope walk.

For two days, the *Maddox* proceeded warily up the coast. Special listening devices installed on the ship for the mission picked up radio messages indicating that the North Vietnamese were monitoring her progress, but no vessel came out to challenge the destroyer as she continued to track and fingerprint Communist radar. Then, on the afternoon of August 2, as the *Maddox* neared one of the islands that had been targeted on July 30, the specialists intercepted a message to three Soviet-made torpedo boats harbored there, ordering them to attack the destroyer. The *Maddox* promptly turned about and headed south at full speed, but her radar operators soon informed the bridge that the torpedo boats were pursuing the destroyer at forty-six knots—nearly twenty knots faster than their quarry. Realizing that the hounds would soon catch the hare, the ship's captain issued a request for air support from the carrier *Ticonderoga*, stationed some 100 miles away off South Vietnam. Shortly after 3:00 p.m., the *Maddox* opened up with her five-inch guns. The North Vietnamese fired a pair of torpedoes, but the *Maddox* dodged them both and soon disabled two of the pursuers with gunfire. Jets from the *Ticonderoga* knocked out the third.

A shell from the USS *Maddox* explodes in the wake of a North Vietnamese PT boat during a skirmish in the Gulf of Tonkin on August 2, 1964. When three PT boats attacked the *Maddox* as it probed North Vietnamese radar defenses, the destroyer replied with its five-inch guns, disabling one boat. This encounter, known as the Gulf of Tonkin incident, triggered a huge U.S. military buildup in Vietnam.

When word of the incident reached Washington, President Lyndon Johnson decided to step up the pressure on the North Vietnamese. A second destroyer, the *Turner Joy*, was sent to join the *Maddox*, and the South Vietnamese continued their coastal raids. On the night of August 3, they shelled a North Vietnamese radar station near the route traced by the *Maddox* a few days before. The following evening, as low clouds settled over the *Maddox* and the *Turner Joy*, radar operators on both vessels began to pick up alarming returns. They may have been ghosts—anomalous signals reflected to the destroyers' antennas from well beyond the horizon by the moisture-laden clouds overhead. Yet the radar operators could not dismiss the possibility that they were reflections from torpedo boats heading for another attack. Time and again, vessels appeared to be approaching from sundry directions, only to disappear from the screen seconds later. "You'd have beautiful pips for a while," recalled radarman James Stankevitz, "and then they'd vanish."

Around 9:30 p.m., radar aboard the *Maddox* indicated that several vessels were closing at forty knots, and the destroyer opened fire. Amid the tumult, the ship's sonarman reported the sound of a torpedo in the water. The *Maddox* took evasive action, weaving back and forth and propagating underwater echoes that jumpy sonarmen evidently mistook for further torpedoes: Twenty-two were reported in all, but the alarms ceased when the evasive maneuvers ended.

When the excitement died down, both ships were undamaged. A preliminary review by the mission commander, Captain John Herrick, aboard the *Maddox*, counseled caution. "Many reported contacts and torpedoes fired appear doubtful," he radioed his superiors. Citing freak weather, an overzealous sonarman, and the absence of

any confirmed sightings of torpedo boats, he recommended a "complete evaluation before any further action." But the initial dire reports from the destroyers had left Washington in no mood to deliberate. On August 5, President Johnson authorized U.S. air strikes against North Vietnam. Three days later the Senate voted overwhelmingly to allow Johnson to take all necessary measures to "prevent further aggression," a resolution that became the basis for committing American troops to the fight in South Vietnam.

The *Maddox* incident highlighted the hazards of entrusting delicate surveillance tasks to ships. Yet unlike aircraft, ships could

Built to foil enemy radars, the Navy's EA-6B Prowler (this one is from the aircraft carrier *Eisenhower*) holds a crew of four: a pilot and three electronic warfare officers, who operate detection and jamming gear contained in the fuselage, in underwing pods, and atop the vertical fin. Wing tanks and the aerial refueling probe jutting from below the windshield allow the Prowler to accompany long-range naval air strikes.

remain on station for days or even weeks. And monitoring radar installed along hostile shores or on enemy vessels was crucial to naval operations in wartime. Part of the job could be performed by land-based aircraft, but the Navy needed elint platforms that were an integral part of its operations to scour electronic data from the immediate environment and route it swiftly to the various commanders.

One alternative to elint by ship was to give aircraft carriers their own electronic surveillance planes. During the Vietnam War, Navy fliers gathered elint from carrier-based EA-3 Skywarriors, twin-engine jets that carried four electronic specialists to monitor data. Late in the conflict, the Skywarriors were joined by a new airborne snooper that remains in service today, the E-2 Hawkeye. A smaller cousin of the E-3 AWACS (Airborne Warning and Control System) then being developed by the Air Force, the Hawkeye is intended primarily to provide early warning of an attack from any direction with radar housed in a revolving dome atop its fuselage. But the Hawkeye also boasts a passive detection system that can ferret out enemy emissions. In Vietnam, this allowed it to cull fresh information about the frequencies used to guide North Vietnamese SAMs and MiGs—data that was translated into countermeasures. The task of applying the ECM during carrier-launched air strikes fell to dedicated electronic-warfare planes such as the EA-6B Prowler. Introduced in 1972, the Prowler had powerful jamming pods that could be programmed to blanket various enemy frequencies.

Although naval elint and ECM were directed mainly at land-based targets in Vietnam, rival fleets remained a prime concern of Navy ferrets elsewhere. Even as Soviet warships grew increasingly sophisticated, they provided more stimuli for electronic sensors. The nuclear-powered cruiser *Kirov*, for example, laid down in 1973, was fitted out with two 360-degree search radars, three navigational radars, six missile-guidance radars, two fire-control radars for its 110-mm cannons, four more for its 30-mm machine guns, and three navigational radars for its helicopters. Ironically, the very systems

Most of the antennas aboard the aircraft carrier *Minsk* (*left*) play roles in controlling the *Minsk's* aircraft and in communicating with the fleet. But, like all Soviet and American warships, the *Minsk* also carries tactical elint antennas that listen for enemy radars—as well as jamming gear to foil them. For example, twin antennas near the bottom of the picture, with surfaces divided into squares, pull in electronic emissions; the pair of disk-shaped antennas below them are jammers.

designed to make such ships more deadly rendered them more vulnerable to jamming or to attack by radar-homing missiles.

The Vietnam era also saw dramatic developments in a branch of electronic surveillance destined to make battlefield snooping less dangerous. Remotely controlled aircraft called drones had played a small part in previous conflicts as offensive weapons, but during the Vietnam War, they came into their own as reconnaissance tools for elint as well as for photography. Premier among these pilotless vehicles was the Firebee, a jet-powered drone weighing about 2,000 pounds. After launch from a Hercules DC-130E transport, the Firebee was flown by technicians operating a console aboard the mother ship; at the end of a mission, the drone cut its engine on command from the DC-130E and deployed a parachute. An orbiting helicopter grappled the canopy and reeled in the Firebee.

In one of the more productive elint operations of the war, the Air Force guided the drones over new North Vietnamese SA-2 missile sites to monitor the SAMs' fire-control radar and relay the data to DC-130Es orbiting at a safe distance. The mission laid the groundwork for a largely successful campaign to counter the SA-2 from the air by launching Shrike missiles that homed on the fire-control radar's operating frequency, destroying the radar.

Encouraged by such results, the United States and other advanced nations have since developed several remotely or internally guided craft—classified together as unpiloted aerial vehicles (UAVs)—for various tactical recon missions (*pages 118-125*). But no country has applied UAVs more resourcefully in battle than Israel during its clash with Syrian forces in Lebanon's Bekáa Valley in the summer of 1982. Having entered Lebanon to root out strongholds of the Palestine Liberation Organization, the Israelis had to contend with a potential counterthrust by Syrian forces concentrated in the Bekáa Valley. Guarding the Syrian tanks and troops there against air assault was a network of nineteen SAM batteries. The Israelis decided to attempt a preemptive air strike, which meant pinpointing the SAM sites, analyzing the characteristics of their fire-control radar, and targeting them with missiles. Intent on minimizing the exposure of their reconnaissance and fighter pilots to the SAMs, Israeli commanders relied on UAVs controlled from ground stations and from an advanced version of the Hawkeye called the E-2C.

The operation began with a photorecon flight by a UAV known as a Scout, which was launched from a truck and carried a television camera monitored from the ground. Built to reflect little in the way of radar energy, the Scout was guided over enemy territory until it located a SAM site. At that point, the ground controllers launched two more compact UAVs—one to fool Syrian tracking radar by emitting a signal like the radar echo of a larger plane and the other to record the emissions of the fire-control radar that the SAM crew would flick on in response to this bogus threat.

The elint thus collected was instantly transmitted to an airborne E-2C, whose computer processed the data. One of three systems operators aboard the Hawkeye then relayed the information to the crew of a U.S.-supplied Phantom jet armed with Shrike missiles, telling them what coordinates to aim for and what signal to seek out. The quick work led to the destruction of seventeen of the nineteen SAM sites in the course of a single afternoon and enabled Israeli pilots to seize control of the skies over the Bekáa Valley at little cost and end the Syrian threat there.

Guarding against the Ultimate Threat

Low-flying drones were not the only pilotless vehicles introduced in recent decades to amass electronic intelligence. Since the early 1960s, satellites have been quietly monitoring radar emissions and missile telemetry from space. At first, the U.S. satellite reconnaissance program concentrated on lifting cameras into space to clear up such strategic questions as the extent of Soviet ICBM deployment. The first elint satellites were thrust into orbit in 1962—two years after the United States began to collect photint in space—and circled earth at an altitude of about 300 miles to pick up long-range Soviet radar signals that would provide early warning of an attack by aircraft or missiles.

Early-warning systems operated almost continuously, enabling the satellites to monitor some frequencies of interest on nearly every orbit. For telint, however, a different approach was needed. Snaring telemetry from Soviet missile tests grew in importance as U.S. intelligence agencies sought to determine not simply how many ICBMs the Soviets had but what new missiles they were developing and how those missiles compared to their U.S. counterparts in terms of range, payload, and accuracy.

By 1972, the United States and the Soviet Union had hammered out the details of a strategic arms limitation treaty (SALT I), but the agreement was filled with loopholes. Although the treaty ruled out increases in the dimensions of launch silos for land-based ICBMs, for example, it failed to prohibit the launching of more powerful missiles with larger payloads from existing silos—an opening the Soviets soon began to exploit with new propulsion techniques. In addition, both nations were developing multiple, independently targeted reentry vehicles (MIRVs), several of which could be packed into one missile and launched from a single silo; the vehicles would then disperse over the target, with each one delivering its warhead to a different spot. Telemetry, in conjunction with other techniques such as multispectral photography of reentering warheads, shed light on these strategic developments by revealing both the composition of the missile's payload and its range and accuracy.

The location and direction of Soviet missile tests could be anticipated; like the United States, the Soviet Union launched test missiles from only a few sites and along prescribed paths. But a satellite sweeping around earth had just a remote chance of being in the right place at the right time to pick up the telemetry. The solution was to elevate spy satellites to a height of 22,300 miles, at which point their orbital rate would equal earth's rotation rate and they could hover above selected areas on the globe. This geosynchronous flight plan required that the satellite carry a big dish to pick up the faint signals from the distant missiles. The first fully operational American orbiter of this class was sent aloft in March 1973 under the code name Rhyolite. On reaching geosynchronous

PINPOINTING TRANSMISSIONS. Rarely seen images from a computer screen reveal the capabilities of airborne radio direction-finding (RDF) equipment. As shown on the map at far right, the aircraft has flown an arc, partly over Israel and partly over the Mediterranean Sea. Dashed lines, representing bearings to a radar taken from four different positions on the plane's path, cross at the location of the transmitter. As the closeup shows, however, RDF bearings rarely cross at a single point, the result of imprecise readings. Taking these discrepancies into account, the computer plots the transmitter as a bright dot in the center of an ellipse where the antenna is almost certainly located. Accuracy is sufficient for directing artillery or calling in air strikes.

orbit high over Borneo, the multipurpose satellite deployed a collapsible antenna some seventy feet wide that took in signals from more than a third of the earth's surface and relayed the data to receivers of similar girth at Pine Gap in central Australia. The system distinguished the telemetry from other signals with the help of a scanner that monitored a frequency band of fifty channels or so that the Soviets employed for such transmissions.

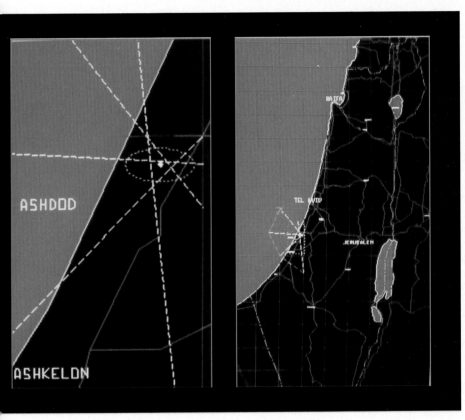

Satellites did not render spyplanes obsolete for telint. For one thing, the Soviets could and sometimes did lower the power of their telemetry in an effort to elude detection from space. But any signal from the missile strong enough to reach Soviet ground controllers could also be picked up by an RC-135 on one of its missile-monitoring flights. For this and other reasons, the workhorse spyplanes maintained their vigil even as U.S. space engineers developed more sensitive receptors. Successors to Rhyolite such as the geosynchronous orbiters of the Magnum series, which entered service in 1985, reportedly possess even larger antennas that may be able to pick up low-power telemetry. Indeed, one antenna recently proposed for development by NASA would be larger than a football stadium and would unfurl like an umbrella in space.

Supplementing satellites and spyplanes are ground-based tracking stations such as the giant Cobra Dane phased-array radar at Shemya. Besides telling Cobra Ball recon crews where to look for telint, Cobra Dane charts a missile's trajectory over time, placing the telemetry in context by revealing exactly how the missile changed course in response to an increase in thrust, for example. Since ground radar cannot detect a missile until it pops up above the station's horizon, dedicated aerial platforms are also needed to spot

Silhouetted against the Alaskan night sky, a 100-foot-high Cobra Dane phased-array radar stands poised to detect Soviet ballistic missiles as they arc toward impact on Kamchatka Peninsula, 450 miles away. Supplementing Cobra Ball flights and other elint missions, Cobra Dane scans the sky with a fixed array of 15,360 electronically aimed transmitters instead of a single rotating antenna. Cobra Dane can spot a basketball-size metallic object in the sky 2,000 miles away and track hundreds of targets at the same time.

the exact time and place of a launch. That task is performed by geosynchronous Defense Support Program (DSP) satellites, which detect the heat of a launch with their infrared sensors.

Aside from its strategic role, DSP made a notable contribution during the Gulf War by detecting the blastoff of Iraqi Scud missiles and alerting U.S. Patriot missile batteries in Saudi Arabia to the incoming threats. The achievement was one part of an exhaustive campaign aimed at amassing intelligence on Iraqi capabilities at invisible wavelengths to complement photographic surveillance and communications intercepts. Bolstered by computerized systems built to monitor and mislead the most sophisticated weapons in the Soviet arsenal, the United States and its coalition partners in the gulf took control of the electronic battlefield in advance and left the Iraqis groping in the dark.

Short-Circuiting Saddam

On August 11, 1990, nine days after Iraqi troops entered Kuwait, a U.S. Air Force RC-135 landed in Saudi Arabia after performing the first flight in a surveillance marathon that would help render the invaders all but defenseless against coalition air power. For the next eight months, at least one RC-135 would be airborne over the region at all times, ferreting out Iraqi radar and communication signals for more than twelve hours at a stretch. The task tested the resources of the 55th Strategic Reconnaissance Wing, which brought only a half-dozen or so RC-135s to the gulf from its home base in Omaha. The Sixth SRW, the other wing flying RC-135s for the Air Force, remained in Alaska to monitor Soviet ballistic missile tests.

The opening months of the vigil were deceptively tranquil for the flight crews and specialists of the 55th. Among the first U.S. servicemen to arrive in the gulf, they lived initially in a Riyadh hotel and traveled to work on a bus that followed a different route every day to guard against terrorist attack. Once aloft, they found the airwaves fairly quiet over Iraq—a sign of good discipline on the part of the Iraqi ground crews, who knew that activating their fire-control radars or defensive communications equipment would only play into American hands. More than anything else, the pilots and navigators in the cockpit and the specialists at their consoles had to fight against boredom and fatigue; with the all-out surveil-

Distant Sentries
for an Early Warning

Since 1971, U.S. Defense Support Program (DSP) satellites have kept a constant watch over the earth's surface from 22,300 miles in space. Orbiting at a rate that matches the earth's speed of rotation, they hover above selected spots on the globe. Their primary duty is to provide first warning of a ballistic missile attack on the United States, but they can also detect tactical missiles, such as the Scuds used in the Gulf War *(overleaf)*, satellite and test-missile launches, and nuclear explosions in the atmosphere. At all times, there are at least three of these sharp-eyed sentinels aloft, and DSP satellites have scored such intelligence coups as giving the West its first notice of the reactor accident at Chernobyl in 1986.

There are three primary DSP satellites and two or more backups aloft. Of the three principal orbiters, one is stationed above the Indian Ocean, scanning the eastern hemisphere from Africa to Australia; it would give first warning of a Soviet or Chinese intercontinental ballistic missile launch. Others over Brazil and the Central Pacific Ocean watch for submarine-launched ballistic missiles.

The satellites' most important intelligence-gathering device is a twelve-foot-long infrared (IR) telescope that focuses an image on an array of IR-sensitive detectors. These sense the energy emitted by a concentrated source of heat, such as a ballistic missile's exhaust plume.

Using IR data from a DSP satellite and computerized memory banks of missile characteristics, analysts on the ground can determine a missile's launch point within three and a half miles, tell what kind it is, and predict its trajectory. "The infrared system we have," an Air Force general summed up, "is the heart and soul of our deterrent posture."

A DSP satellite is thirty-three feet long and weighs 5,200 pounds. Solar panels covering the fuselage and four paddles provide power to run sensors and other equipment. Besides an infrared telescope *(retracted here)*, a DSP satellite has detectors for gamma rays and other radiation that help distinguish a nuclear explosion from other hot spots.

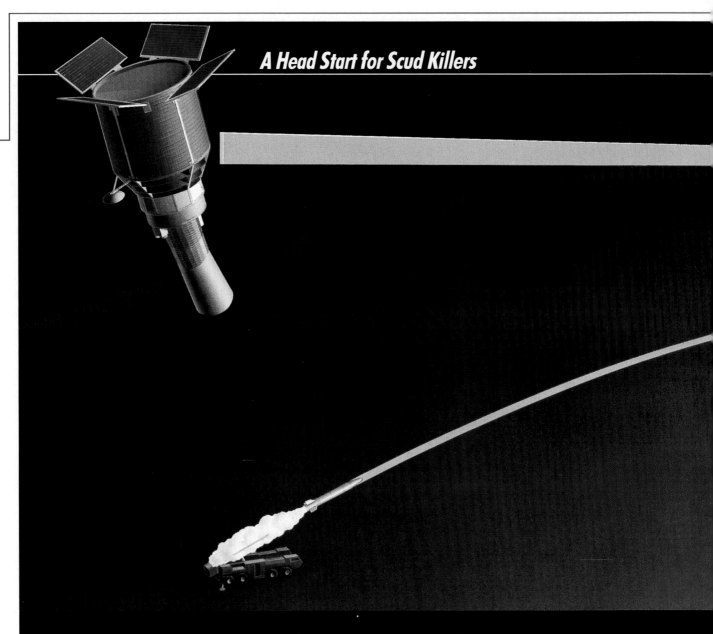

During Operation Desert Storm, the DSP satellite orbiting above the Indian Ocean provided early warning of Scud missiles fired from Iraq. Within one minute of a launch, the observation post transmitted digitized infrared images of the missile's exhaust plume to the U.S. Space Command's Missile Warning Center in Colorado Springs, Colorado *(green arrow)*. Space Command analysts judged that the heat came from a Scud. That information, along with the direction of flight and where the missile would hit, was flashed to the appropriate Patriot missile battery in the war zone *(blue arrow)*. Thus alerted, the Patriot system picked up the Scud on its fire-control radar and loosed a missile at it. From Scud launch to the time the Patriot battery fired took two minutes, five minutes less than the Scud's deadly journey.

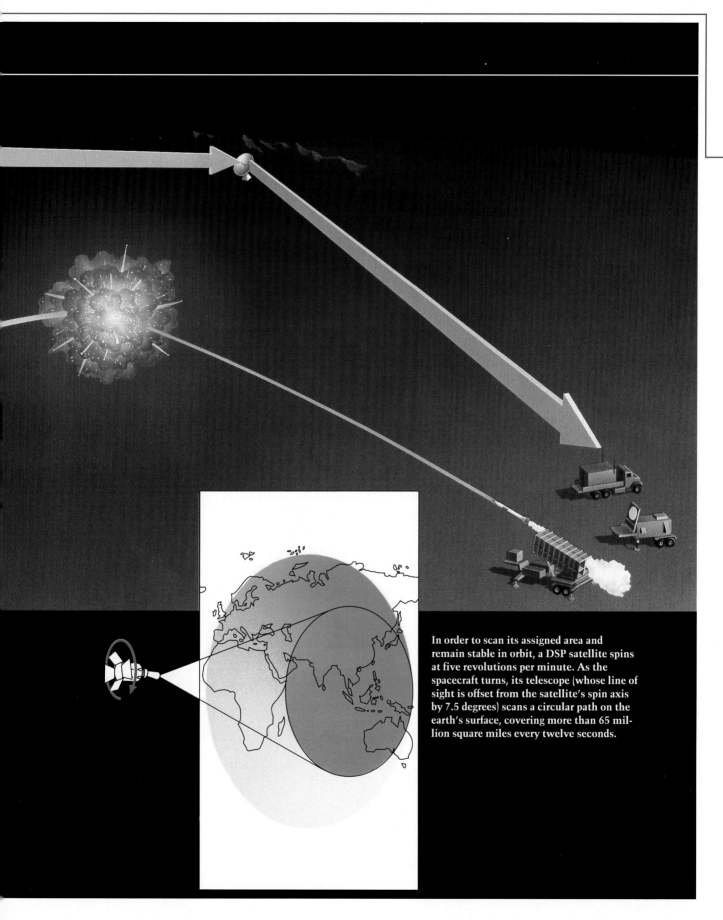

In order to scan its assigned area and remain stable in orbit, a DSP satellite spins at five revolutions per minute. As the spacecraft turns, its telescope (whose line of sight is offset from the satellite's spin axis by 7.5 degrees) scans a circular path on the earth's surface, covering more than 65 million square miles every twelve seconds.

lance effort, there were no backup crews on board to spell them.

In time, the persistence of the patrols and the pressure placed on the Iraqi crews by months of heightening tension yielded results. As war loomed, big strike packages of coalition aircraft formed up regularly and made feints toward Iraq, inciting the wary defenders to break their electronic silence. "The Iraqis were good," observed one pilot who logged more than 200 hours over the gulf in command of an RC-135, "but they weren't good enough." Lapses by the enemy and keen detection by the RC-135s and other ferret planes added significantly to the library of available data on Iraqi air defenses. The United States already knew the broad frequency range of the predominantly Soviet-supplied radar systems that warned the Iraqis of air strikes and guided their interceptors, SAMs, and antiaircraft artillery; the ferret flights helped narrow the band to be searched so that it could be covered by the scanners on the various jamming pods and antiradar missiles carried by U.S. warplanes.

Shortly before Operation Desert Storm began, in mid-January, the new data was programmed into the memories of many of those devices—a process that could take anywhere from a few hours to several days, depending on the system. With vintage equipment, black boxes or pods had to be removed from planes and reconfigured, but more advanced ECM gear could be reprogrammed on the aircraft simply by attaching a cable from a portable computer and copying the fresh data into the system's memory. The programming told the system not only what part of the electromagnetic spectrum to scan but how to distinguish enemy radar signals within that band from inoffensive transmissions. By constantly checking signals against its memory bank, which included the distinctive fingerprints of the various enemy systems, the computer could identify the threat and select the appropriate response instantaneously.

This preparation paid off in the opening moments of the air campaign launched against Iraq on January 17. Among the planes waging electronic warfare that night were Air Force EF-111A Ravens and Navy EA-6B Prowlers with computerized jamming systems that could analyze and counter transmissions from up to twenty radar installations simultaneously. Supporting the pilots on both planes were electronic warfare officers (EWOs), who could modify the jamming program if the Iraqis resorted to unforeseen frequencies or pulse-repetition rates. But the coalition's success in hitting hundreds of targets deep inside Iraq that night while losing only four aircraft—less than one percent of the total strike force—suggests that the Iraqi defenders largely followed the anticipated script.

Lieutenant Fred Drummond, an EWO for one of the Navy Prowlers, characterized the effect of the jamming on the enemy radar operators: "They might think it is a malfunction to start with. We know that from training our own people. They see their screen as being whited out, there's large strobes coming across it. By that time they know that something is coming at them, but they don't know at what altitude or direction." If the frustrated ground crews continued to operate their sets, they were easy prey for antiradar missiles launched by F-4 Phantoms. The combined effect of the two countermeasures—missile strikes and jamming—was to stifle Iraqi air defenses in short order. On the first night, nearly 100 Iraqi radar installations responded to the allied air strikes. Within a few weeks, the number was down to about a dozen.

Fittingly for an air campaign that relied as much on technological finesse as on raw firepower, one of the first Iraqi warplanes to go down in the war was a French-built F-1 Mirage that was outmaneuvered by an unarmed EF-111A. Spotted by the Mirage while his plane was conducting jamming on January 17, the Raven pilot, Captain Jim Denton, dived to within a few hundred feet of the ground, where the EF-111A could take full advantage of its superb terrain-hugging navigation system. The Iraqi pilot followed suit, but he was out of his element. "We got so low he couldn't hack it," explained the Raven's EWO, Captain Brant Brendon, "and he smeared into the ground behind us."

More important than such individual triumphs was the chilling effect of the ECM on the Iraqi Air Force as a whole, which declined to put up more than token resistance without an effective ground radar network that would allow the outclassed Iraqi interceptors to gang up on opponents. Looking back on the campaign, Lieutenant General Charles Horner, the supreme air commander of the coalition, cited the quick suppression of enemy defenses on the first night as the turning point. "When we got through those first ten minutes," he remarked, "we knew we had 'em. It was only a matter of time." This swift and stunning breakthrough was years in the making, however. Behind those ten minutes lay decades of research and reconnaissance that enabled the United States and its allies to dominate the airwaves and deny the enemy electronic guidance when it mattered most.   ★

Robots for
Overhead Surveillance

In the high-tech world of electronic spies, safety ordinarily lies in moving fast and operating from a distance. But one means of intelligence collection is different, taking a close approach and a lingering look. It makes use of the flying robots known as unmanned aerial vehicles, or UAVs.

The first systematic use of unmanned planes for reconnaissance came in the Vietnam War. During that conflict, such aircraft flew 3,500 missions. Although the low-risk harvesting of intelligence was appreciated, UAVs stirred no great enthusiasm until 1982, when the Israelis put on a dazzling display in the Bekáa Valley of Lebanon using pilotless aircraft to stimulate a reaction by Syrian SAM radars and to pinpoint their locations. This intelligence

helped the Israeli Air Force wipe out nineteen missile sites and then, free to roam the skies, destroy eighty-six enemy aircraft, losing only one plane in the process.

Inspired by this example, other nations began developing UAVs. The accelerated evolution has yielded rich variety: diminutive craft resembling model planes, grander machines that can travel far and remain aloft for long periods, rotary-wing craft able to take off and land anywhere. Most can be piloted from the ground by radio, and some also function as drones, following courses programmed into the guidance systems before launch. Their sensors range from simple video cameras to sophisticated radars and infrared detectors. Their missions can include moni-

toring enemy movements; spotting targets; assessing bomb damage; detecting the use of chemical, biological, or nuclear weapons; jamming radars; and much more.

Dozens of UAVs are now in service or under development. The example seen above, the experimental CM-44, has a twenty-nine-foot wingspan and a turbocharged engine at the rear to push it along. Cruising at 210 miles per hour, 25,000 feet above the ground, it can carry a 600-pound payload of sensors, and it can be programmed for flights lasting up to eighteen hours. This UAV and the three others shown on the following pages suggest the scope of current efforts to give field commanders a ready source of intelligence with no human risk.

A No-frills Design for Close-in Work

For simplicity and ease of use, no UAV excels the graceful craft called the Pointer *(right)*, which is designed to supply a field commander with a picture of what lies just beyond his field of vision. As one admirer says, "It gives you the high ground, no matter where you are. It makes you 500 feet tall with a set of binoculars."

In essence, the Pointer is a rugged, all-electric version of a radio-controlled model airplane. Although it has a nine-foot wingspan and is six feet long, it weighs only nine pounds. Two men can carry the plane and its control gear in backpacks, and they can assemble and launch it in just four minutes.

By means of a trailing antenna wire, the Pointer receives commands from its operators and sends back television images of the world below as it circles or explores at a typical operating altitude of 500 feet. Detection by the enemy is unlikely because of its small size and the nearly inaudible whir of its battery-powered motor.

The low cost, portability, and simple design of the Pointer are powerful advantages, but they exact a price in the capabilities of the system. For example, maximum range is about five miles, the limit of the radio-control transmitter. Battery charge holds endurance to a little over an hour. Lack of a navigation system complicates use of the Pointer, especially over terrain with few distinctive features, such as the desert battlegrounds of the Persian Gulf War. That conflict revealed another shortcoming: Strong desert winds and thermal currents sometimes flung the little Pointer about, limiting its tactical utility.

Requiring no runway or launcher, the Pointer can be sent aloft either from a moving vehicle or by a single man running and then heaving it into the air *(left)*. The earthbound pilot *(right)* peers into a television monitor while a second operator *(background)* keeps the image sharp by adjusting an antenna. The pilot maneuvers the radio-controlled craft with a joystick like those used to fly free-flight model airplanes.

A tiny television camera *(above)* carried in a fixed position in the Pointer's nose is identical to commercial 8-mm models except for a rugged protec-

High-resolution television images of the target area, in color or black and white, are received instantly. Pictures—the one above was taken at

Longer Reach and Sharper Eyes

For pilotless reconnaissance beyond the range of the pint-size Pointer, U.S. forces in the Persian Gulf War relied on a twelve-foot-long, 420-pound UAV called the Pioneer—here seen streaking skyward with a rocket assist. Pioneers were aloft every minute of the war, beaming live television and infrared images to their operators by day and night. They proved their worth early by detecting Iraqi probes near Khafji, Saudi Arabia, in the first significant ground battle. But surveillance was only one of many missions assigned to them: They served as target spotters for air strikes and naval gunfire; they were used to hunt mines; and they searched out control bunkers, antiaircraft artillery batteries, and SAM sites.

Equipped with a satellite-aided navigation system, the Pioneer has a maximum range of 100 miles, can transmit its images from an altitude of 15,000 feet, and is able to loiter over an area of interest for six hours. Versatility, however, brings trade-offs in convenience. The UAV requires a crew of about twelve, and where a runway is lacking, the Pioneer needs a special rail for launch and a net to snare the craft at the end of the mission.

Marines in Saudi Arabia ready a Pioneer for launch from an inclined rail—the method used when no suitable runway is available on land or when the UAV is dispatched from a ship. Based on Israeli UAV designs, the stubby, twin-boomed craft has a seventeen-foot wingspan and can carry a 100-pound payload. A rocket below the fuselage gives the Pioneer's twenty-six-hp piston engine a needed boost on takeoff.

To retrieve the Pioneer at sea or when a runway is lacking on land, an operator throttles the vehicle down from its top speed of ninety-two miles per hour and guides it into a net. During the war in the Persian Gulf, forty Pioneers were deployed to units of the Army, Navy, and Marine Corps, and more than 300 missions were flown.

Crew members use a crane to swing a Sentinel from a truck to its takeoff platform, which has its own batteries and devices to feed navigation information to the aircraft from the mobile ground-control station *(right background)*. The squat cylindrical transmitter in the trailer *(far left)* sends the radio signals that control the vehicle in flight.

A Gift for the Vertical

Among the many designs for UAVs currently being explored, the peanut-shaped Sentinel is perhaps the most exotic. A robotic helicopter, it has some clear advantages over fixed-wing craft such as the Pointer or the Pioneer: Besides being able to take off and land almost anywhere, it can hover over a point of interest for a long, steady look.

In its upper module, the five-foot-tall, 400-pound Sentinel has a 51.5-hp turbine engine that drives two rotors; they rotate in opposite directions to keep the craft from spinning. The lower module holds a payload of up to 100 pounds, consisting of a TV camera, radar, infrared sensors, or even electronic-warfare gear. Traveling at more than eighty miles per hour, the Sentinel has a range of forty-two miles when piloted by remote control but can venture as far as seventy-five miles from its takeoff point when operating as a drone. It can reach an altitude of 10,000 feet and maintain an electronic vigil for as long as four hours.

Whether or not the Sentinel becomes operational, it possesses a virtue likely to be sought in all future UAVs: It is stealthy. The downwash from the rotors cools the exhaust, minimizing the chances of being shot down by heat-seeking weapons. And a short, curvy fuselage built mostly of nonmetallic materials reduces the flying peanut to a tiny blip on radar screens.

Inside the control station, the Sentinel operator *(foreground)* guides the vehicle during flight with the joystick directly in front of him. The payload operator *(background)*, controls the cameras and other sensors.

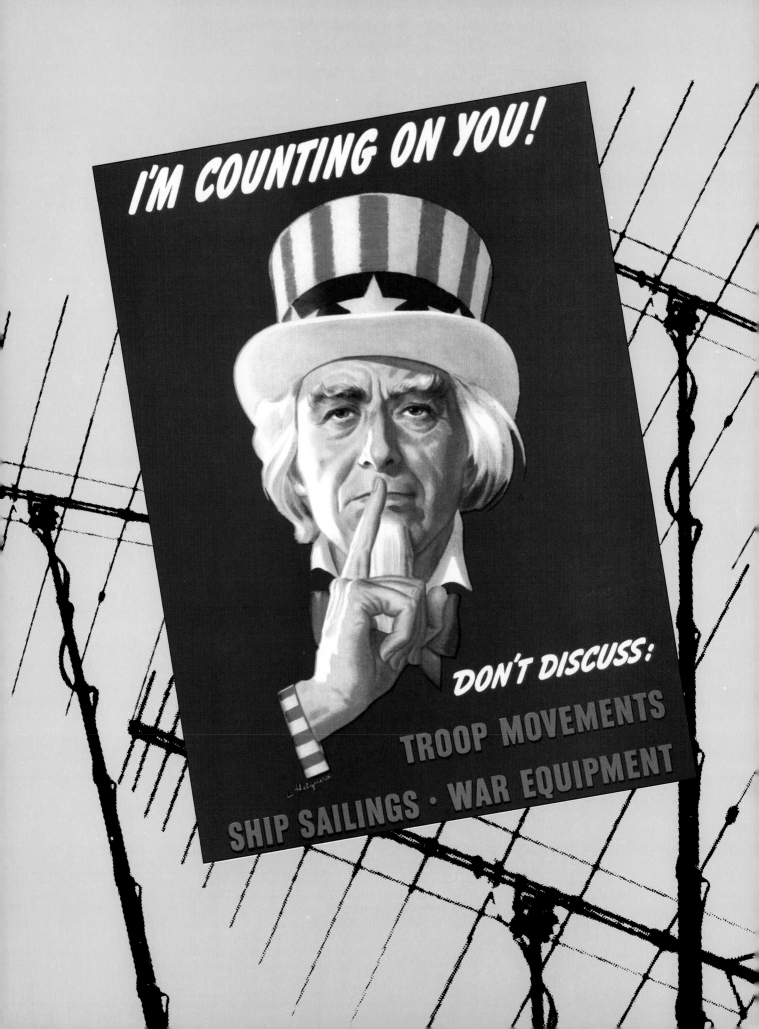

Eavesdroppers Extraordinaire

Among the many antennas crowding the roof of the U.S. embassy in Moscow in the late 1960s was one with a special, top-secret function. With it, technicians from the National Security Agency could pull in signals from the car phones of Soviet leaders as they chatted with each other while riding around the city. Unlike today's cellular systems, portable phones of that era used a single frequency, so it was simply a matter of finding the right one and listening in. The Soviets, with misguided aplomb, did not bother to scramble or encode their conversations.

The intelligence gleaned in this way was not of a high strategic order—"We didn't find out about, say, the invasion of Czechoslovakia," said a former U.S. official—but it did provide insight into Soviet leaders' health and personal habits, about which little was otherwise known. It was also an excellent method of keeping tabs on their whereabouts and learning who was meeting with whom.

The project—code-named Gamma Gupy—worked well until September 1971, when newspaper columnist Jack Anderson revealed that the United States had "for years been eavesdropping on the most private conversations of Kremlin leaders. For obvious security reasons, we can't give a clue as to how it's done." He did not have to; the Russians needed only to know that they were victims. They added scramblers—devices that break audio signals into jumbled digital bits and then reassemble them at the other end—to the car phones, and the intelligence from Gamma Gupy dried up overnight.

But that was not the end of the story. In 1987, Assistant Secretary of Defense Richard Perle testified to Congress that a year after Anderson's disclosure, the U.S. embassy in Moscow was still picking up the mobile conversations. The Soviets, certain that their voice communications were now secure thanks to the scramblers, would sometimes go beyond the usual small talk, but American code breakers had managed to defeat the devices. In this way, the

127

United States overheard a highly sensitive discussion between Leonid Brezhnev and his defense minister concerning the deployment of new SS-19 nuclear missiles. This intelligence windfall, too, was finally compromised, not by the press but by an intelligence specialist who was promoted into a position that gave him access to the Gamma Gupy intercepts. He later admitted to being a Soviet spy.

Communications intelligence, as it applies to war and foreign policy, is the practice of intercepting others' confidential messages, including not only the personal phone calls of a nation's leaders, but intragovernmental memos, diplomatic instructions, military radio traffic, as well as the communications of anyone—terrorist groups, for example—whose actions might jeopardize a country's security. Though the way that messages are transmitted—and intercepted—has changed greatly over the years, one aspect of this clandestine activity has remained constant: the overriding need for secrecy. If an enemy knows that his communications are being read by the other side, he may change codes, switch to other channels, or even plant false information knowing it will be picked up. Yet properly handled and protected, communications intelligence, or comint, can be invaluable in assessing an enemy's intentions. While photint and elint can reveal the extent of a country's military assets, comint can furnish clues as to how—and, indeed, whether—the leaders who control those weapons plan to use them.

In the United States, one organization—the National Security Agency—has been responsible for compiling, interpreting, and disseminating comint since 1952. When President Harry Truman signed a top-secret directive creating the agency, he ended a long history of frustrating turf wars in the comint community. Like medieval fiefdoms battling for territory, the Air Force, Army, Navy, Coast Guard, State Department, CIA, and FBI had all staked claims—some of them overlapping—to portions of the communications intercept field. There was no overall structure for handling the intelligence that each agency might clandestinely acquire.

Technologically, the United States was among the best at intercepting and deciphering foreign coded messages, but the system of getting the finished intelligence product to the proper recipient in a timely manner was cumbersome and haphazard. In 1941, this muddled state of affairs would figure in the greatest tragedy in American military history, but the origins of the U.S. comint community's predicament had arisen more than a decade earlier.

In 1929, after two months on the job as President Herbert Hoover's secretary of state, Henry Stimson was handed a batch of decoded Japanese diplomatic cables. Until then he had not known of the existence within his own State Department of an office—intriguingly called the Black Chamber—that deciphered foreign cable traffic provided by cooperative American telegraph companies. Convinced that such an operation had no place in the diplomatic arena, he promptly axed the program's budget. Later, he summed up his feelings on the subject in a sentence that has become celebrated in the comint trade, "Gentlemen do not read each other's mail."

The Black Chamber's operations were transferred to the new Signal Intelligence Service (SIS) of the U.S. Army Signal Corps. By establishing the SIS, the Army provoked a decade of rivalry with an already-existing Navy bureau, known as OP-20-G, that was also in the signals-intercept business. Assessing their operations, a review board later concluded, "The method of processing and disseminating the diplomatic messages that were read was both duplicative and unseemly." SIS and OP-20-G ultimately reached a peculiar compromise; the Navy handled diplomatic intercepts on odd-numbered days, the Army on days with even numbers. Equally troublesome was the almost paralyzingly high security accorded this intelligence. Intercepted messages were carried by hand to the appropriate official, who read the document in the courier's presence and then gave it back. As a result, there were no copies to go astray but neither was there a simple way for the official to refresh his memory of something he had read earlier. Though in desperate need of overhaul, the system would require a massive shock to set the wheels of change in motion.

In the early-morning hours of December 7, 1941, a Navy listening post on Bainbridge Island, near Seattle, intercepted several messages from Tokyo to the Japanese embassy in Washington, D.C., and relayed them to OP-20-G headquarters. The gist of the messages was ominous: Japan's ambassador was told to terminate negotiations with the U.S. government at precisely 1:00 p.m. and destroy cipher equipment. Navy analysts realized the significance of the specified hour immediately—one o'clock Washington time would be early Sunday morning in Hawaii, with military readiness at its lowest point. Because of comint, the Americans held in their hands an unmistakable warning of impending hostilities.

Two officers scurried frantically around Washington with the intercepted messages, briefing every top official they could find. By 11:00 a.m., Army Chief of Staff George Marshall had read the news and grasped its meaning. He had to alert the military commander in Hawaii but hesitated trusting such sensitive information to the scrambler-phone connection for fear the Japanese, playing their own comint game, might learn that their codes had been compromised. He gave the warning instead to the War Department for encoded radio transmission and was assured that it would arrive in Hawaii in less than thirty minutes. Atmospheric conditions, however, were playing havoc with radio circuits to Hawaii that day, so the message was encoded and sent by commercial teletype. Instead of thirty minutes, it arrived an hour and forty minutes later—a mere twenty minutes before Japanese planes appeared over Pearl Harbor. Even the loss of an hour left enough time to put the island on alert, but no one had stamped the message urgent. At the telegraph office, it was put in the box marked routine delivery, finally—and uselessly—reaching the commanding general's office some eight hours after the attack.

In the heartbreaking aftermath, Secretary of War Henry Stimson, the man who had banished comint from the State Department more than a decade earlier, now called for a thorough review of comint practices. Stimson was a convert; he knew that, in the present circumstances, the United States needed every advantage its technology and ingenuity could provide. Too little attention had been paid to routing intercepted cable traffic to its proper destination quickly, he charged. Stimson's review led to the creation of the top-secret Special Branch within the War Department. This office would become the sole evaluator and analyzer of comint from all sources. It was a wartime expedient that served America well.

With this improvement over the previous parochial system, the United States derived much success from intercepted enemy communications, including forewarning of Japanese plans to invade Midway Island. This knowledge greatly facilitated American victory in the decisive naval battle of the Pacific war. Admiral Isoroku Yamamoto's intention to visit a forward base in 1943 was also laid bare, affording the Americans an opportunity to lay an ambush for him and shoot his plane out of the sky, thereby killing Japan's premier naval strategist.

Undoubtedly the most famous comint coup of the war belonged to America's ally Great Britain, which succeeded in cracking Nazi Germany's most secret ciphers. Shortly after war broke out in September 1939, the British managed to obtain a working example of a German encryption device called Enigma. Mere possession of the machine, however, did not permit its new owners to read German military wireless traffic. Enigma's complicated wiring, connected by a series of rotors, could spin out an extraordinarily complex cipher. Without the correct key—a string of numbers changed frequently by the Germans and used by all Enigma operators to set up the machines for both encoding and decoding—the cipher lay beyond human capacities to solve.

But a team of British cryptologists from the Government Code and Cypher School found a way of deciphering Enigma traffic electronically. Their device could justifiably be called the world's first computer, an invention that would, over the years, become indispensable to code makers and breakers. This technological breakthrough enabled the British to listen in on communications between U-boats at sea and the German Admiralty. It also revealed the targets of upcoming Luftwaffe raids on Britain and clued the British in to Rommel's plans in North Africa. The Allies used the information—code-named Ultra—circumspectly lest the Germans infer that Enigma had been compromised. Throughout the war and long afterward, Ultra remained a well-kept secret.

In 1943, the British combined several comint operations into one department, the Government Communications Headquarters (GCHQ), which still controls all such activities. The United States would ultimately create a similar agency, but not without further bureaucratic bickering. Late in the war, the Army and Navy formed a joint Communications Intelligence Board at President Franklin D. Roosevelt's insistence, but the Navy, again fighting turf wars, was loath to cooperate. Then, in 1949, responsibility for comint passed to the Joint Chiefs of Staff. This move only perpetuated the interservice rivalry that had existed since 1929 and extended it to the recently independent Air Force. In December 1951, the

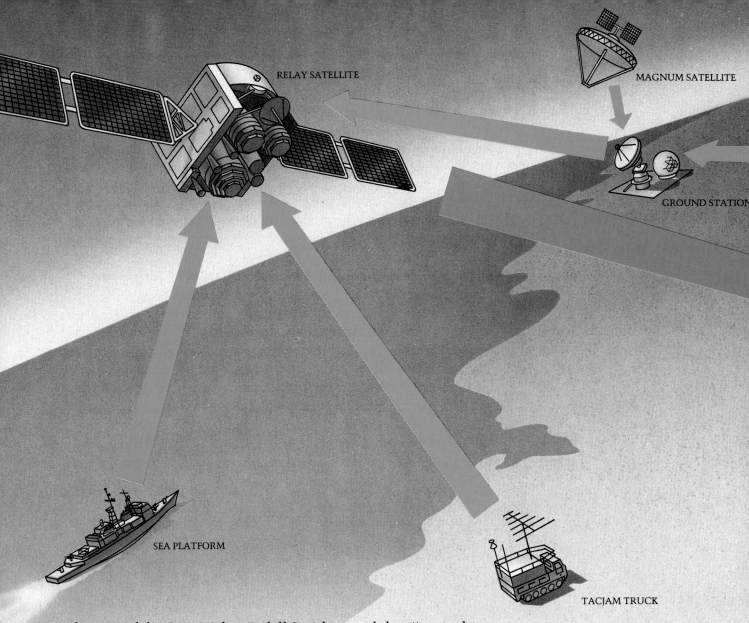

RELAY SATELLITE

MAGNUM SATELLITE

GROUND STATION

SEA PLATFORM

TACJAM TRUCK

director of the CIA, Walter Bedell Smith, stated that "control over, and coordination of, the collection and processing of Communications Intelligence have proved ineffective." This bleak assessment of the U.S. comint function, largely unchanged after almost a quarter century, precipitated a basic change. Henceforth, all such operations would be consolidated under one roof.

The Puzzle Palace

No proclamation accompanied the birth, on October 24, 1952, of the National Security Agency (NSA). Unlike the CIA, it was not created by statute. President Truman signed the NSA into being with an eight-page, top-secret directive entitled Communications Intelligence Activities, and for the next five years, the U.S. government did not even acknowledge its existence. For organizational purposes, the document placed the new agency, "within, but not part of, the Department of Defense." This apparent contradiction is

A Communications Network for Communications Intelligence

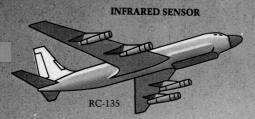

INFRARED SENSOR

RC-135

National Security Agency headquarters at Fort Meade, Maryland (below), is the ultimate destination of communications intelligence gathered by intercept stations around the world. Virtually all such information—whether it is gathered by a satellite, a mobile or fixed ground station, a ship, or an aircraft—reaches headquarters by way of one or more relay satellites. In the majority of cases, the trip from a remote installation to Maryland takes less than one second.

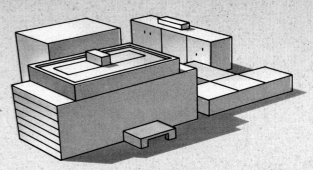

NATIONAL SECURITY AGENCY

in actuality a clever ploy that enables the NSA to conceal its operating costs within the mammoth defense budget. Another effect has been to reduce substantially the interservice rivalries that once seemed to undermine the American comint effort.

In good budgetary times and bad, the NSA thrives. The behemoth of the U.S. intelligence empire, it is headquartered at Fort George G. Meade on a thousand secluded acres in the Maryland countryside between Washington and Baltimore. Some 45,000 employees commute daily to the complex of buildings, which is surrounded by a double cordon of chain-link fence ten feet high and topped with razor wire, with a high-voltage electric fence in between. In a basement underneath the main building, the world's greatest concentration of advanced computer systems, several thousandfold more powerful than the device that cracked Enigma, extends for the equivalent of several city blocks. In all, the NSA sets aside approximately eleven acres of space for its computers.

The agency is divided into four primary operational sections. The Office of Telecommunications and Computer Services, which is known in the intelligence community as T Group, maintains this multimillion-dollar array of electronic equipment. It also provides secure channels of communication between NSA headquarters and the agency's far-flung listening posts, and transcribes intercepts for cryptologists and translators to convert from gibberish into English.

Home for the scientists who are constantly searching for new and better ways of prying into another country's secrets, the Office of Research and Engineering, or R Group, encompasses both the practical and the theoretical. While engineers work on new designs for antennas and listening devices, mathematicians study probabilities and statistics for new code-breaking solutions.

An important NSA mandate is to make America's secret communications impenetrable to outsiders. The Office of Information Security, S Group, designs encryption equipment for the armed forces and the State Department to use in their worldwide communications nets. It has been rumored that this division tests its newly devised gear against the NSA's own code breakers. "That was what we were supposed to do," said a former NSA director, "but I wasn't technically oriented enough to know whether, in fact, we did do it." S Group also oversees the installation of secure voice links and computer terminals throughout the federal government, a substantial responsibility. In 1984, for example, S Group began a nationwide program to provide encrypted telephone service to a half a million government employees.

Largest of the NSA branches, and the nerve center of U.S. comint collection, is the Office of Signals Intelligence Operations, called P Group after its former name, the Office of Production. It contains the linguists, cryptologists, and intelligence analysts who spy on the world's communications traffic. Even in the post-Cold War era, the former Soviet Union remains a principal target because of its nuclear arsenal, but no country on earth—from the staunchest ally to the most insignificant banana republic—is immune to P Group's eavesdropping. There is a wide variety of platforms at P Group's disposal for obtaining data. The agency controls the activities of a substantial quantity of military assets—ranging from spyplanes and satellites to a worldwide network of giant antennas on the ground—with which it scoops up the raw material of the trade.

P Group also has responsibility for the agency's communications network—dubbed SPINTCOM, for special intelligence communications. Information from throughout the NSA empire is relayed by satellite to two huge dish antennas at Fort Meade. By way of a three-quarter-mile cable, the signals are fed into the NSA's message-interpreting hub. For the most urgent transmissions, a special network, CRITICOM, is used. Its job is to send a CRITIC, a special message of such urgency that it must reach the president and other top officials within ten minutes. In this way, the NSA hopes to ensure that the nation never again suffers the intelligence problem it had at Pearl Harbor, when vital information was intercepted but didn't get where it needed to go in time.

NSA operations can be classified by the platform involved. Aircraft are as convenient for communications intelligence as they are for other types of information gathering. Trying to draw a reaction from air defenses for later analysis, American comint planes have often flown directly at—and sometimes across—the Soviet border. The missions produced useful information about the response of Soviet air defenses to such incursions, but the dangerous game sometimes carried a high cost.

On September 2, 1958, an EC-130 on an NSA mission went down in Soviet Armenia with the loss of all seventeen crewmen. NSA eavesdroppers on the ground, who were monitoring Soviet Air Force frequencies, listened helplessly to the chatter of MiG pilots as they closed in, then blasted the EC-130 out of the sky. Between 1950 and 1969, the Russians fired on a total of twenty-three American aircraft and shot down twelve.

Their allies sometimes reacted with equal hostility. On April 15, 1969, a Navy EC-121, flying from an air base near Yokohama, Japan, and carrying thirty-one crewmen and technicians, was shot down by North Korean interceptors. In the aftermath, further comint flights in the region were stopped. So vital was the intelligence gained from these missions, however, that they were soon reinstated—with fighter escort.

Aside from vulnerability, the chief disadvantages of aircraft for such surveillance were lack of range and endurance. Regions such as central and southern Africa, for example, were impractical targets for aircraft, and many lay beyond the range of ground stations as well. A partial answer seemed to lie in ships, which can sail long distances and remain on station for weeks at a stretch. Moreover, the Soviets had been using a fleet of so-called fishing boats off the coasts of the United States and elsewhere for several years. With prominently protruding antennas, these seagoing platforms fooled no one about their mission, but they made good spies. They looked nonthreatening—at least in a naval combat sense—as they tailed warships and trolled near sensitive military installations, hauling in signals rather than fish. One 600-ton Soviet trawler, for instance, was an inconspicuous electronic witness to the testing of the first U.S. nuclear submarine equipped with a Polaris missile.

The first American spy ship was the USS *Private José F. Valdez*, a former troopship retrieved in 1960 from the mothball fleet of the U.S. Maritime Administration and outfitted with sensitive radio receivers. Owned and operated by the NSA over the objections of the U.S. Navy, the *Valdez* was dispatched to cover the emerging nations of sub-Saharan Africa. Even though ships generally cannot intercept signals originating deep within the interior of a continent, the one-ship fleet returned a trove of valuable information.

With that success on the record, the Navy changed its opinion of oceangoing vessels as comint platforms and joined in plans for a second generation of spy ships. Under the deal struck with the NSA, the Navy would man and operate the vessels, and though Fort Meade would have first call on their services, naval intelligence authorities could otherwise employ them to gather whatever information they wished. In 1962, one of these ships, loitering off the coast of Cuba, picked up the first credible indication of Soviet nuclear missile deployments, a development later confirmed photographically by U-2 overflights.

Duty aboard a spy ship seemed safe compared with charging to-

ward hostile air defenses in an aircraft. Lightly armed and slow, the vessels gave target nations ample opportunity to confirm that they posed no threat. As long as they remained in international waters, there appeared to be little justification for an attack, either accidental or intentional. As events would prove, however, this was a faulty calculation.

A Case of Unmistaken Identity

The USS *Liberty* was a converted World War II vessel that had been recommissioned for spy service in 1964. In 1967, with tensions rising between Israel and her Arab neighbors in the Middle East, the *Liberty* was pulled from patrol duty off the West African coast and hurriedly sent to the Mediterranean. The change of assignment stemmed from a request by the NSA to the Joint Chiefs of Staff, which then issued the requisite orders through the military chain of command. In Spain, the ship took on supplies and six Arabic linguists flown in by the NSA. While in port, the crew learned something of the communications setup east of Suez from the USS *Valdez*, which had just steamed slowly through the Suez Canal, listening all the way. The *Valdez*'s intelligence cache detailed "who was communicating on what links—teletype, telephone, microwave, you name it," an NSA official later recalled.

On June 5, as Israel launched air strikes against Egypt, Syria, and Jordan to open the Six-Day War, the *Liberty* was passing Sicily's southern coast, heading east. By the time she arrived on station—a point just 13 miles off the coastal town of Al-'Arīsh in the Sinai—the war was in full swing and the eastern Mediterranean had emp-

Soviet intelligence-collection ships, poorly disguised as fishing boats, long have listened in on American communications. The one at left cruises off the coast of Hawaii in December 1988 as an AWACS aircraft lands at bustling Hickam Air Force Base and the nuclear attack submarine *Sam Houston* heads into Pearl Harbor. Other "trawlers" regularly loiter near large U.S. military facilities such as the naval complex at Norfolk, Virginia.

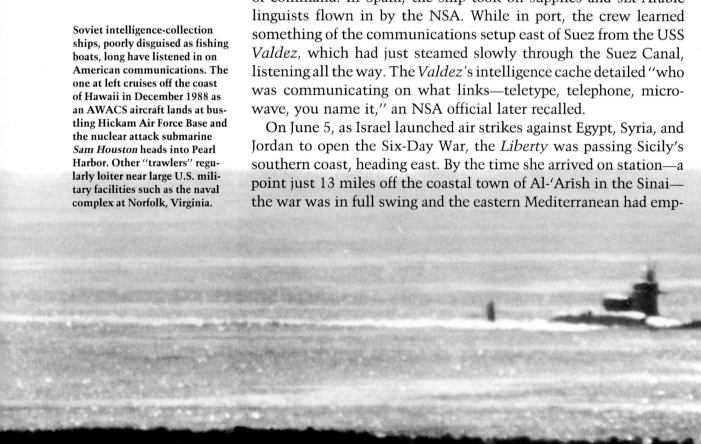

munications, are all well and good. For a battalion commander in a fight, however, the information they provide is yesterday's news. For that reason, battalion commanders have comint resources of their own.

Included among these resources are linguists to translate enemy communications, but radio conversations need not be understood to be informative. It is helpful simply to know that a transmitter is active or units ranging in size from a platoon to a theater headquarters.

If the transmitter is within range of artillery—or if a couple of fighter-bombers can be dispatched—the enemy officers guiding the battle can be killed, with the potential of severely hampering the opposition. Or a similar effect can be had simply by flooding enemy frequencies with electronic noise to drown out their transmissions.

In an exercise at Fort Huachuca, Arizona, a radio-direction-finding team attempts to get a bearing on an opposing transmitter. Drawn as straight lines on a map, this bearing and one from a second team dispatched to a different po- sition form an X that marks the location of the transmitter. Such assignments can be hazardous, often requiring that teams take up exposed posi- tions well forward of their friends in order to ob- tain an accurate fix.

This **TACJAM** (Tactical Jamming) system is used to disrupt enemy communications. Built into a box that can be secured to the bed of a truck or a tracked chassis, as shown here, the system has a telescoping antenna for intercepting messages; it can be retracted when the vehicle is on the move. The conical antenna on the short mast is for sending jamming signals. Inside the box resides a computer system and several transmitters that can monitor and disrupt a number of channels at the same time.

tied of ship traffic. The *Liberty* was alone. Among themselves, the officers somberly discussed the inherent danger of their close proximity to a war zone. There were second thoughts in Washington, as well. Late on June 7, the Pentagon ordered the *Liberty* to withdraw first 20, then, hours later in a subsequent message, 100 miles from the Sinai. Because of communications difficulties, however, neither message reached the ship and the *Liberty* continued to steam slowly on a course parallel to the coast.

During the morning of June 8, the *Liberty* was buzzed several times by low-flying Israeli military aircraft—cargo planes that had been converted for reconnaissance work. Israeli jet fighters also circled overhead. The *Liberty*'s U.S. flag stood straight out from the mast in a stiff breeze. Her identification symbol—GTR 5—was conspicuously painted in white letters ten feet high on the hull.

Moments after 2:00 p.m., with the *Liberty* plainly in international waters a good fourteen miles from shore, Israeli Mirage and Mystère fighter-bombers streaked in just above the waves. Without warning, they unleashed a devastating barrage of rockets, then returned for a second pass with napalm. Fire engulfed the *Liberty*'s superstructure, the antennas, masts, and radar disappearing in a ball of flame. The planes continued their attack, relentlessly strafing the burning ship and perforating the deck with more than 800 fist-size holes. Then, presumably out of ammunition, they vanished as quickly as they had come.

A few minutes later, Israeli torpedo boats appeared, firing 20-mm and 40-mm guns. Next, they loosed a salvo of torpedoes at the *Liberty*. One passed behind the ship, but a second struck the forward hull at the site of her comint compartment. The explosion tore a forty-foot hole in the *Liberty*'s side and killed many of the ship's communications experts. Incessant gunfire from the torpedo boats shredded rubber life rafts as sailors tried to put them into the water. Miraculously, the riddled and burning *Liberty* did not sink.

Although the Israelis were jamming communications, the crew—using jury-rigged radio gear—managed to send an SOS to the U.S. Sixth Fleet, which sent two destroyers to provide escort. The battered, blood-soaked ship limped into harbor at Malta. Thirty-four Americans had died and two-thirds of the crew had been wounded.

The next day, Israel offered apologies, claiming that it had mistaken the 10,680-ton, 455-foot *Liberty* for a 2,460-ton, 275-foot Egyptian transport called the *El Quseir*, which was, at the time of the attack, docked in the Egyptian port of Alexandria. Given the frequent overflights by Israeli planes that morning as well as the *Liberty*'s prominent markings and clearly visible flag, this explanation is unconvincing. It is hard to imagine the attack as anything but a deliberate effort to keep a U.S. listening post from eavesdropping—legally—on military transmissions from the battle fronts.

On the day of the attack, Israel had almost completed its lopsided, victorious campaign over three Arab foes. Conquest of the West Bank of the Jordan River and of the Sinai was assured, but the Golan Heights, deemed essential to Israel's principal war aim of achieving defensible borders, remained in Syrian hands. Strategic national interest, therefore, dictated that the extent of Israel's gains—and the dire circumstances of its enemies—stay hidden until this last, vital piece of territory had been captured, lest the superpowers step in to halt the fighting.

Israeli Defense Force press releases underplayed the Army's success, and the Arabs were loath to admit publicly the magnitude of their defeat, but the *Liberty*'s electronic ears could deduce the true nature of the situation. Thus, as naval historian Richard Smith wrote, "any instrument which sought to penetrate this smoke screen so carefully thrown around the normal 'fog of war' would have to be frustrated." Israel's leaders knew the potential consequences of a ruthless strike on a vessel belonging to its closest ally. That they chose to proceed demonstrates how sensitive and unforgiving even a friendly nation can be when it feels a threat to its security, whether from gun barrels or radio receivers.

Though the Israelis' proffered explanation was lame, the U.S. government chose to swallow it. Accepting an apology, monetary compensation for the wounded and the families of the dead, and a paltry six million dollars for damages to the thirty-million-dollar ship (which was decommissioned and sold for scrap), the United States swept the incident under the rug. Anything, apparently, was better than casting a public light on intelligence activities that involved the supersecret NSA.

Only seven months later, a second U.S. spy ship would come to grief in an episode that changed the complexion of America's efforts at seagoing comint collection. The USS *Pueblo*, a converted tramp steamer, and two sister ships were American versions of the ubiquitous Soviet trawlers. The *Pueblo*'s maiden comint voyage was a Navy mission; she was to "sample the electronic environment of the east coast of North Korea and intercept and conduct surveillance of Soviet naval units operating in the Tsushima Straits."

Naval intelligence analysts assessed the risk of this mission as minimal. One NSA employee, who received an information copy of the *Pueblo*'s tasking order, disagreed. The Communist government of North Korea was known to be belligerent and unpredictable, and unlike the Soviet Union, it had no snooping trawlers of its own. Thus, there could be little confidence that it would tolerate the presence of U.S. spy ships. A warning message flashed from Fort Meade to the Pentagon emphasizing that the North Koreans showed little respect for international maritime law and implying that the *Pueblo*'s assignment should be reconsidered. Sticking by its own estimate of the danger, the Navy let the mission proceed.

On January 23, 1968, the *Pueblo*'s captain, Commander Lloyd Bucher, had his ship at rest sixteen miles from shore, well beyond the twelve-mile strip of coastal sea that the North Koreans claimed as territorial waters. When a Russian-built North Korean submarine chaser—a fast, well-armed patrol craft—approached, Bucher ordered his intelligence officer belowdecks to find out if it was possible to eavesdrop on any talk with her base. Said Bucher: "It might be fun to know her impressions of us."

It soon became clear that the subchaser was at general quarters—battle stations—and that three torpedo boats were also advancing. Bucher still wasn't overconcerned—harassment was a standard part of the spy game at sea—but when the Korean ship signaled "Heave to or I will fire!" he realized this was no ordinary encounter. Bucher sent a message to his headquarters at Sasebo Naval Base in Japan warning of possible trouble. Knowing it would take two hours either to scuttle the ship or to destroy all classified material aboard, he ordered what he later termed a dignified withdrawal.

Bucher's adversaries, however, outnumbered and outgunned his tiny ship, and they could more than match its twelve-knot speed. As the *Pueblo* got under way, the North Koreans repeated their warning, then the subchaser suddenly opened fire with its 57-mm cannon. Machine guns on the torpedo boats joined in. Aboard the *Pueblo*, sailors were burning classified material as fast as they could. "It was frustrating to discover how incombustible large amounts of paper can be," the commander later recalled.

Bucher was frustrated, too, by the failure of the ship's own specialists to help divine its attackers' intentions. Two Marine Corps linguists aboard were monitoring the North Korean ships' communications. Said one of them, according to Bucher: "It's nothing but a lot of fast gibberish which we can only identify as Korean. We're just not proficient enough at the language, sir."

One last message from the *Pueblo* before its capture declared: "Four men injured and one critically and going off the air now and destroy this gear." The critical injury became a fatality, and the remaining eighty-two *Pueblo* crewmen were arrested, interrogated under torture, and imprisoned for eleven months under the harshest conditions. America's intelligence system had suffered, too. From the smoky interior of the *Pueblo*, the North Koreans salvaged a working KW-7 encryption machine—S Group's state-of-the-art device for communicating with NSA facilities.

The days of defenseless U.S. spy ships were over. Seagoing comint operations in the future would be undertaken by heavily armed destroyers and frigates, specially outfitted with communications-intercept gear. Vessels like *Liberty* and *Pueblo* had proved too vulnerable to hostile attack to warrant the risk to their crews. Other platforms, both orbiting and earthbound, would take up the slack.

The first satellite designed to collect communications intelligence was called Rhyolite. In 1970, the first such spacecraft, described as "half the size of a freight car," was placed in a geosynchronous orbit over the Horn of Africa. From this spot it could scan the western Soviet Union, including two test ranges for strategic missiles. Soon, a second was parked over the island of Borneo, from where it could cover the entire Asian mainland. Once in place, each satellite unfurled a seventy-foot-wide dish antenna capable of intercepting the narrow, pencil-beam transmissions of microwave traffic within the Soviet Union. The signals they received were beamed down to the NSA's supersecret listening facilities at Menwith Hill in England and Pine Gap near Alice Springs in the interior of Australia.

Although positioned more than 20,000 miles above the earth, Rhyolite satellites, later renamed Aquacade, were sensitive enough to intercept ordinary radio and telephone conversations originating in the Soviet Union and China. More recent comint satellites, code-named Vortex and Magnum, are thought to be capable of picking up signals from low-power transmitters like the walkie-talkies common among the world's police forces.

Their skipper, Commander Lloyd Bucher, in the lead, the crew of the comint ship USS *Pueblo* marches through the streets of Pyongyang, North Korea, on January 23, 1968. Although more than two hours passed between the North Korean seizure of the vessel earlier the same day and its arrival at the port of Wonsan, no rescue attempt was mounted. Aircraft that might have helped were either improperly equipped for a rescue mission or out of range.

144

The existence of the top-secret Rhyolite was, like the Gamma Gupy program before it, betrayed by a spy in 1981. Christopher Boyce, who worked for TRW, the prime contractor for the satellite, sold details of the system to the Soviets—to little effect. Short of knocking the satellite out of orbit, not much can be done to evade its acute hearing. It is always listening, ready to take advantage of the slightest lapse in communications discipline.

Listening posts on the ground can range in size and complexity from an inconspicuous van parked on a city street to the Edzell station in Scotland, used for eavesdropping on ships, which boasts enormous concentric arrays of antennas ranging from 8 to 100 feet in height and covering an area the size of three football fields. Some of these facilities are unmanned, operated by remote control. Such an installation typically has scanners that continuously check par-

ticular frequencies or channels for some signal other than the hissing, crackling noise commonly heard between radio stations. Upon hearing one, the scanner automatically activates a tape recorder that records the message. Every hour or two, the tapes are electronically relayed to a master site, either a larger NSA field station or the agency's headquarters at Fort Meade.

A large, manned facility typically might feature a host of specialists, divided either by the targets they monitor or by the type of communications they track. A high-priority choice, for example, might be frequencies of the Soviet Union's Navair communications system, used by all military aircraft except fighters. Remarkably, radio operators in the Navair system still tap out Morse code for their transmissions, a technique abandoned decades ago by most air forces. Some twenty-four to thirty-six specialists could be monitoring dots and dashes on different frequencies, and several others listening to voice communications related to other activities. The voice operators have special language training—not just in the classroom style, but in listening to actual, static-filled transmissions over headsets and transcribing the gist of their contents. In a sense, even Morse code operators must be linguistically proficient, because each nation has its own Morse code idiom. And even within a country, there may be one special Morse code lexicon, for example, for maritime messages and another for air defense, while still others might be employed by tank or infantry companies.

This "elephant cage" comint antenna at Chicksands Royal Air Force Base, England, is duplicated in Scotland, Japan, China, and other sites. Consisting of three concentric antenna rings, each optimized for a different frequency band, the array is overseen by a large computer at the center. By noting the differences in arrival times of a signal at individual antennas in a ring, the computer can judge the bearing to the transmitter with an error of less than five degrees.

Typically, there are three tiers of analysts. A first-phase analyst has fully honed language proficiency and expertise on a very specific target—a particular Soviet air regiment of fifty aircraft, for example. The analyst would know each of the regiment's pilots by name, call sign, and the tail number of his plane. A second-phase analyst, in turn, might be well versed on an entire military district's Air Force units, while a third-phase analyst, up the line, may be more attuned to the overall national air-defense structure. In addition to their routine surveillance, stations are often asked to be on the lookout for particular information of interest to analysts somewhere who are seeking to solve an intelligence puzzle. During the Vietnam War, for example, reports surfaced that the Russians were whisking captured American pilots out of North Vietnam for interrogation in the Soviet Union. Consequently, the NSA tasked its Soviet Air Force specialists to watch for clues—in aircraft flight patterns and radio traffic—that might confirm the story.

The picture of the NSA as an agency that exploits every possible opportunity to gather communications intelligence from land, sea, air, and space becomes complete with an unusual mission code-named Ivy Bells. The Soviets had laid an underwater cable across a narrows at the northern end of the Sea of Okhotsk, between the Kamchatka Peninsula and the Siberian mainland. Often used for military communications—including data from ballistic-missile tests—the cable was considered so secure because of its location in

what amounted to Soviet waters that the Soviets often did not bother to encrypt messages they sent across it.

Sometime during the late 1970s, U.S. Navy divers, operating from a submarine, fastened to the cable a pod with a wraparound device that tapped into the cable without touching the wires inside it. The pod contained a tape recorder that recorded messages on various channels for several weeks. Divers periodically retrieved the take and returned it to the NSA for study. Moreover, the pod was designed to fall away if the cable was raised for maintenance or inspection, keeping the secret safe—at least until 1981, when it was divulged by a spy named Ronald Pelton, a former NSA employee. Shortly thereafter, the Soviets greatly increased their naval activity in an apparent effort to discourage further American submarine visits, bringing an end to a daring comint enterprise.

A Worldwide Game

The preeminence of the British among spies in fiction and film is not just a coincidence. Their nation excels in espionage, and comint is no exception. In the years after World War I, when the American Black Chamber was gearing up, prior to its run-in with Secretary Stimson, the British ruled the world's telegraph system. Because of the extent of the British Empire, virtually all the world's international messages passed along a British cable at some point. With the authority of the Official Secrets Act of 1920, the British simply eavesdropped on them all, commercial as well as governmental.

During World War II, Britain and the United States became not just military allies, but comint partners as well. In 1940, even before America entered the conflict, Prime Minister Winston Churchill appealed to President Roosevelt for an exchange of technical information. In 1943, the two nations joined in a formal bilateral understanding that provided for high-level comint cooperation and standardized security procedures. That partnership endures to this day in the UKUSA Agreement, signed in May 1947—a pact whose existence has never been acknowledged by either government.

Close cooperation, however, has been something of a mixed blessing. Secrets about the Rhyolite satellite were betrayed not only by Christopher Boyce, but also by a GCHQ employee named Geoffrey Arthur Prime. Prime had joined the British comint agency in

Computerized databases have become essential to virtually every kind of military enterprise, from distributing payroll to logging the ins and outs of spare parts for tanks and aircraft. Keeping track of intelligence data is no exception. Information about an opponent that makes the rounds in the form of documents is slow to travel and time-consuming to collate into a meaningful picture. Indeed, it is not uncommon for an important piece of the puzzle to be overlooked, forgotten, or submerged in a sea of papers on an officer's desk.

One solution is for intelligence gatherers to enter information into a common electronic database, one that can be shared by all of the commanders who make decisions about an action. Not only do all these officers then see and make judgments on identical information, but the computer never forgets anything. New information is automatically incorporated into the picture—shown on a monitor in the form of an annotated map—just as soon as it appears in the database.

Programmed appropriately, the computer can automatically place enemy and friendly units on the map, outline threat areas around antiaircraft defenses, and even suggest to commanders which of all the possible targets are in the most urgent need of destruction.

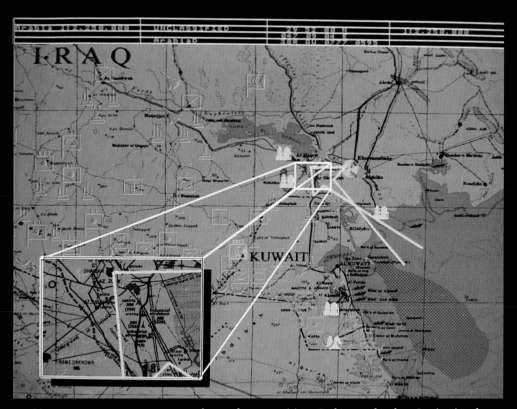

A blue arrow on a computer-generated map of Kuwait and southern Iraq marks the target: Shaibah air base near Basra *(inset)*. Besides airfields *(red planes)*, this simulation shows information gathered by a variety of means, especially photography and electronic intelligence. Comint provided little data; the Iraqis communicated largely by buried cable. Scallops along the Kuwaiti border mark Iraq's forward troop positions. Red rectangles show Iraqi units of various types and sizes. Those with red dots in the center, for example, are chemical units. A SAM site looks like a small hummock with three lines shooting from the top. The pink flag just north of the scallops is the Iraqi headquarters for the Kuwait Theater of Operations, while the pink rosette farther north is a nuclear reactor. Yellow symbols stand for oil refineries.

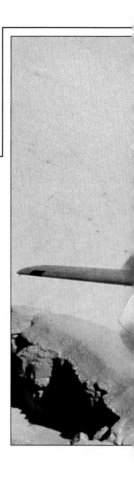

1968 after serving in the Royal Air Force and rapidly rose through the ranks. During this time, he supplied classified information to the Soviets, including, at some point, the details of the Moscow embassy-based Gamma Gupy project as well as the Rhyolite.

The UKUSA Agreement does not prevent mutual spying. By one account, this provides a way to identify lapses. But the two nations' wills may clash, as they did in the 1956 Suez crisis, when the United States knew of an otherwise-secret British and French plan for military intervention because it had broken its friends' codes. Recalls one NSA veteran: "I was one of a whole team of men whose only job was to read and process intercepted British communications."

Britain's empire may have waned, but its interest in comint has never ceased. During the war in the Falkland Islands in 1982, a Foreign Office official caused embarrassment when he openly informed the House of Commons that his government "had been reading the Argentines' diplomatic traffic for years."

Land-based listening stations are also operated by other NATO allies and by Japan and China. Third World nations generally have a limited ability to undertake sophisticated eavesdropping operations; furthermore, they often rely on commercial cipher firms to provide the equipment to safeguard their official communications. But technological limits do not always stop them. In the Gulf War, for example, not all the comint action was on the winning side. The Iraqis monitored coalition radio transmissions with Soviet and Western electronic equipment to learn about the air tactics being used against them and to develop countermeasures. Despite their decisive defeat overall, Saddam Hussein's forces enjoyed some small successes. U.S. analysts learned of one such accomplishment through their own comint—eavesdropping on Iraqi radio traffic. They heard the commander of a mobile Scud missile launcher telling his superior well before the arrival of attacking aircraft that he was making a fast exit from the area because "F-16s are coming after me." The analysts' conclusion: The Iraqis had broken the allied target-coding system so that listening in on forward air-traffic controllers could tell them which specific targets were to be hit.

When U.S. pilots talked among themselves about how to evade Iraqi radar-guided, surface-to-air missiles, the Iraqis overheard. They learned, for instance, that the pilots reacted to the SA-8 Gecko missile with a hard turn into its flight path at a right angle, followed by another hard turn toward the missile when it came near. This

maneuver sometimes succeeded in breaking the missile's radar lock because the SA-8 could not turn quickly enough. The Iraqis responded by using the shorter-range, SA-14 Gremlin heat-seeking missile at right angles to their SA-8 batteries. The heat plumes created by the pilots' sharp turns could draw the second missile.

The biggest potential threat to allied success in the gulf, however, came from Soviet, not Iraqi, intelligence. Mikhail Gorbachev publicly supported the U.S.-led coalition's campaign to remove the Iraqis from Kuwait. But some American officials feared that hardliners in the Kremlin or the Soviet military might alert Saddam Hussein to his opponents' preparations for the lightning armor assault that would overwhelm his army. Evidently, the fear was groundless. Radio intercepts showed the Iraqi dictator had no idea what confronted him.

Silent cooperation of this kind is new in Soviet-American intelligence activities. The USSR maintains a vast spying and codebreaking system, and U.S. facilities worldwide have always been the top target. American officials contend that all satellite-relayed telephone calls in the southeastern part of the country now can be intercepted by a giant Soviet listening post in the Cuban town of Lourdes near Havana. A twenty-eight-square-mile complex, comprising some fifty buildings and including large dish antennas installed in 1977, can pull in signals from more than 100 U.S. communications satellites.

SOVIET COMMUNICATIONS INTELLIGENCE FACILITY
LOURDES, CUBA

ANTENNA FIELDS

SATELLITE RECEIVERS

SOVIET HEADQUARTERS

Eight years earlier, the two superpowers signed an agreement for the construction of new embassies in each other's capitals. The Soviets had the foresight to choose a site high on a Washington hill with an unobstructed line of sight to several of the microwave relay towers that carry the capital's telephone traffic. The Americans, on the other hand, actually turned down a lofty embassy site for one of the lowest spots in Moscow because it was more convenient to government buildings and the ambassador's residence.

When construction began in 1979, things got worse. A cocky U.S. government knew the Soviets would try to lace the building with listening devices but let Soviet factories make precast concrete pieces for the building anyway, confident that U.S. technical experts could neutralize the bugs. That confidence was misplaced.

"We found cables in the concrete," one U.S. engineer reported. Electronic packages had been inserted where steel reinforcements belonged. Inside concrete columns and steel beams, there were interconnecting systems that would have allowed the Soviets to monitor both electronic and verbal communications. Chillingly, the Americans, not fully understanding the technology of these sys-

This base in Lourdes, Cuba, largest Soviet listening post outside the Soviet Union, can eavesdrop on military, space, and commercial communications in the United States. The picture above, taken by a high-flying American aircraft in 1983, shows antenna fields that monitor ground communications and satellite receivers that spy on space communications.

152

tems, could not disable them. Ultimately, in 1985, Soviet workers were barred from the construction site, but a State Department study showed that razing the building and putting up a new one would be cheaper than debugging the existing structure.

Meanwhile, the old embassy was having trouble, too. The KGB had managed to plant electronic devices in thirteen of the embassy's IBM Selectric typewriters. Each key sent a recognizable instruction to the typing ball as it sped across the page. The bugs transmitted the typing signals to nearby receivers, where they were recorded for later reconstruction into the text of sensitive documents. Worse was what happened to the embassy's communications programs unit, or CPU—a twenty-by-thirty-foot steel vault located in a secure part of the building. After a 1987 spy scandal involving Marine guards at the embassy—in which one man received a twenty-five-year sentence for espionage—the CPU was brought back to the United States to be dissected and examined by NSA technicians, using x-ray, spectroscopic, and infrared analysis.

It turned out that circuit boards in some of the computerized equipment had been replaced in Moscow without U.S. knowledge, perhaps providing the means for the Soviets to filch confidential foreign-policy communications before they had been encrypted for transmission or after they had been decoded upon arrival. Also, the CPU's daily cipher keys may themselves have been copied—compromising not just the Moscow embassy, but U.S. embassies around the world. It was a fiasco of epic proportions but, like the attack on the *Liberty*, was downplayed by the government and buried as much as possible. "There's a cover-up to hide embarrassment," explained an intelligence official.

Neither the thaw of *glasnost* nor the disintegration of the Soviet Union is likely to halt the manifold activities of comint by and between the major players. But the Third World and its dangers loom proportionally larger in U.S. thinking than they have in the past. Training the NSA's considerable assets on the illegal narcotics trade, for example, might give U.S. enforcement officials a much-needed advantage in stemming the flood of drugs across the border. With the international arms trade bustling and many arms purchasers unpredictable, there is a continuing need to know what leaders and armies are saying to each other. The NSA and the other players in worldwide comint show no signs of giving up the game—however ungentlemanly—of reading others' mail. ★

Acknowledgments

The editors wish to thank the following for their assistance: Guy Aceto, *Air Force Magazine*, Arlington, Va.; Lt. Col. James V. Bertrand, Pennsylvania Air National Guard, Middletown, Pa.; Richard M. Bissell, Jr., Farmington, Conn.; Nate Boyer, EOSAT, Lanham, Md.; Lt. Gen. James R. Brickel (Ret.), Oakton, Va.; Duncan Campbell, London; Maria Fede Caproni, Rome; M. Sgt. Perry Champ, Beale Air Force Base, Calif.; Ray Coleman, Unmanned Aerial Vehicle Joint Project, Arlington, Va.; Bill Cox, Autometric Inc., Alexandria, Va.; Dorothy Cross, Pentagon, Washington, D.C.; Alessandro Di Blase, Meteor S.p.A., Ronchi dei Legionari, Italy; Lorna Dodt, Pentagon; David and Tamir Eshel, Hod Hasharon, Israel; Giancarlo Fre, Alenia S.p.A., Rome; Col. Michael Gallagher, Ramstein Air Base, Germany; Sheldon A. Goldberg, Bolling Air Force Base, Washington, D.C.; Capt. John Grevin, Bergstrom Air Force Base, Tex.; Douglas N. Grize, Cirrus Technology Inc., Nashua, N.H.; William Heimdahl, Bolling Air Force Base, Washington, D.C.; Hugh Howard, Pentagon; Jacopo Jacopozzi, Agenzia Imago, Rome; Col. Lawrence Krull (Ret.), Barrington, Ill.; Anthony LeVier, Lockheed Advanced Development Co., Burbank, Calif.; Dan London, VITec, Vienna, Va.; Carroll Lucas, Autometric Inc., Alexandria, Va.; John B. Marks, Loral Fairchild Data Systems, Arlington, Va.; Maj. Doug Martin, Pentagon; Irene Miner, Pentagon; Lyle Minter, Pentagon; Hugh Morgan, Dayton, Ohio; Clark Nelson, SPOT Image Corp., Reston, Va.; Michael D. Normansell, Charlottesville, Va.; M. Sgt. Steven P. Pagel (Ret.), Woodbridge, Va.; Maj. Terry Pappas, Edwards Air Force Base, Calif.; John Pike, Federation of American Scientists, Washington, D.C.; David Pincus, Martin Marietta, Littleton, Colo.; James W. Ragsdale, Lockheed Advanced Development Co., Burbank, Calif.; William Rosenmund, Pentagon; Gus Slayton, Association of Old Crows, Alexandria, Va.; Richard B. Stadler, Lockheed Advanced Development Co., Burbank, Calif.; Mabel Thomas, Pentagon; Maj. Lou Tiedemann, Langley Air Force Base, Va.; Sedgwick Tourison, Crofton, Md.; Capt. James F. Tynan, George Air Force Base, Calif.; Paolo Valpolini, Milan; Susan Vassallo, Grumman Corp., Bethpage, N.Y.; Peter Zimmerman, Georgetown University, Washington, D.C.; Capt. Jeffrey Zuress, Bergstrom Air Force Base, Tex.

Bibliography

BOOKS

Aart, Dick van der, *Aerial Espionage: Secret Intelligence Flights by East and West.* Transl. by Sidney Woods. New York: ARCO/Prentice Hall Press, 1986.

Armitage, Air Chief Marshal Sir Michael, *Unmanned Aircraft.* New York: Brassey's, 1988.

Ball, Desmond, *Soviet Signals Intelligence (SIGINT).* Canberra, Australia: Australian National University, 1989.

Bamford, James, *The Puzzle Palace.* New York: Penguin Books, 1983.

Berger, Carl, ed., *The United States Air Force in Southeast Asia, 1961-1973.* Washington, D.C.: Office of Air Force History, 1984.

Bolger, Daniel P., *Americans at War.* Novato, Calif.: Presidio Press, 1988.

Bucher, Comdr. Lloyd M., and Mark Rascovich, *Bucher: My Story.* New York: Doubleday, 1970.

Burrows, William E., *Deep Black.* New York: Random House, 1986.

Crickmore, Paul F., *Lockheed SR-71 Blackbird.* London: Osprey Publishing, 1986.

Davis, Brian L., *Qaddafi, Terrorism, and the Origins of the U.S. Attack on Libya.* New York: Praeger, 1990.

De Arcangelis, Mario, *Electronic Warfare.* Poole, Dorset, England: Blandford Press, 1985.

Donald, David, *Spyplane.* Osceola, Wis.: Motorbooks International, 1987.

Dorr, Robert F.:
Air War Hanoi. New York: Blandford Press, 1988.
McDonnell F-101: Voodoo. London: Osprey Publishing, 1987.

Drendel, Lou, *SR-71 Blackbird in Action.* Carrollton, Tex.: Squadron/Signal Publications, 1982.

Dutton, Lyn, et al., *Military Space.* London: Brassey's, 1990.

Ennes, James M., Jr., *Assault on the Liberty.* New York: Random House, 1979.

Fitts, Lt. Col. Richard E., ed., *The Strategy of Electromagnetic Conflict.* Los Altos, Calif.: Peninsula Publishing, 1980.

Francillon, René J., Peter B. Lewis, and Jim Dunn, *Electronic Wizards.* London: Osprey Publishing, 1991.

Friedman, Col. Richard S., et al., *Advanced Technology Warfare.* London: Salamander Books, 1985.

Futrell, Robert F., *The United States Air Force in Korea 1950-1953.* Washington, D.C.: Office of Air Force History, 1983.

Gunston, Bill, *An Illustrated Guide to Spy Planes and Electronic Warfare Aircraft.* New York: Prentice Hall Press, 1983.

Hallion, Richard P., and the Editors of Time-Life Books, *Designers and Test Pilots* (The Epic of Flight series). Alexandria, Va.: Time-Life Books, 1983.

Jensen, John R., *Introductory Digital Image Processing.* Englewood Cliffs, N.J.: Prentice-Hall, 1986.

Johnson, Clarence L. "Kelly," and Maggie Smith, *Kelly.* Washington, D.C.: Smithsonian Institution Press, 1985.

Johnson, Nicholas L., *The Soviet Year in Space, 1990.* Colorado Springs, Colo.: Teledyne Brown Engineering, 1990.

Jones, R. V., *The Wizard War.* New York: Coward, McCann & Geoghegan, 1978.

Kennedy, Col. William V., *Intelligence Warfare.* New York: Salamander Books, 1983.

Kessler, Ronald, *Moscow Station.* New York: Charles Scribner's Sons, 1989.

Lindsey, Robert, *The Falcon and the Snowman.* New York: Pocket Books, 1979.

Lo, C. P., *Applied Remote Sensing.* Harlow, Essex, England: Longman Scientific & Technical, 1986.

Martin, David C., and John Walcott, *Best Laid Plans.* New York: Harper & Row, 1988.

Meyer, Mark, *Wings.* Charlottesville, Va.: Thomasson-Grant, 1984.

The Military Frontier, by the Editors of Time-Life Books (Understanding Computers series). Alexandria, Va.: Time-Life Books, 1988.

Miller, Jay, *Lockheed SR-71 (A-12/YF-12/D-21)*. Austin, Tex.: Aerofax, 1983.

O'Leary, Michael, and Eric Schulzinger, *Black Magic*. Osceola, Wis.: Motorbooks International, 1989.

Peebles, Curtis, *The Moby Dick Project*. Washington, D.C.: Smithsonian Institution Press, 1991.

Powers, Francis Gary, and Curt Gentry, *Operation Overflight*. New York: Holt, Rinehart and Winston, 1970.

Richardson, Doug:
Electronic Warfare. New York: Prentice Hall, 1985.
Stealth. New York: Orion Books, 1989.

Richelson, Jeffrey T.:
American Espionage and the Soviet Target. New York: William Morrow, 1987.
America's Secret Eyes in Space. New York: Harper & Row, 1990.

Richelson, Jeffrey T., and Desmond Ball, *The Ties That Bind*. Boston: Allen & Unwin, 1985.

Russell, Francis, and the Editors of Time-Life Books, *The Secret War* (World War II series). Alexandria, Va.: Time-Life Books, 1981.

Sabins, Floyd F., Jr., *Remote Sensing: Principles and Interpretation*. New York: W. H. Freeman, 1986.

Shaker, Steven M., and Alan R. Wise, *War without Men*. New York: Pergamon-Brassey's, 1988.

Simonsen, Erik, *U.S. Spyplanes*. Poole, Dorset, England: Arms and Armour Press, 1985.

Stanley, Col. Roy M., II, *World War II Photo Intelligence*. New York: Charles Scribner's Sons, 1981.

Taylor, John W. R., and David Mondey, *Spies in the Sky*. New York: Charles Scribner's Sons, 1972.

Ulanoff, Brig. Gen. Stanley M., and Lt. Col. David Eshel, *The Fighting Israeli Air Force*. New York: Arco Publishing, 1985.

West, Nigel, *The SIGINT Secrets*. New York: William Morrow, 1986.

Windchy, Eugene G., *Tonkin Gulf*. New York: Doubleday, 1971.

Woodward, Bob, *Veil*. New York: Pocket Books, 1987.

Yenne, Bill, *Lockheed*. New York: Crescent Books, 1987.

Yost, Graham, *Spy-Tech*. New York: Facts On File Publications, 1985.

PERIODICALS

"Almost Astronauts." *Air Force*, October 1990.

Anderson, Casey, "Return of the Blackbird?" *Air Force Times*, February 11, 1991.

Aviation Week & Space Technology, April 22, 1991.

Baker, Caleb, and George Leopold, "Gulf War Takes Toll on Pioneer UAVs." *Defense News*, March 18, 1991.

Bird, Julie, "Jammers Cutting Anti-Aircraft Risk." *Air Force Times*, January 6, 1991.

Brugioni, Dino A., "Naval Photo Intel in WWII." *U.S. Naval Institute Proceedings*, June 1987.

Burrows, William E., "Space Spies." *Popular Science*, March 1990.

"Canadair to Resume CL-227 Flights after Completing Technical Review." *Aviation Week & Space Technology*, May 15, 1989.

Charles, Daniel, "Spy Satellites: Entering a New Era." *Science*, March 24, 1989.

Cockburn, Andrew, "Sixty Seconds Over Tripoli." *Playboy*, May 1987.

Dornheim, Michael A., "U.S. Reconnaissance Weakened by SR-71 Program Termination." *Aviation Week & Space Technology*, January 11, 1990.

Dugdale, Don, "Tapping the EW Potential of Unmanned Air Vehicles." *Defense Electronics*, October 1986.

Elachi, Charles, "Radar Images of the Earth from Space." *Scientific American*, December 1982.

Elmer-Dewitt, Philip, "Inside the High-Tech Arsenal." *Time*, February 4, 1991.

"Enhancing Images from Space." *International Defense Review*, May 1991.

"Flying the Big Black Bird." *Airman*, October 1970.

Fromm, Joseph, "Trigger-Happy Soviets." *U.S. News & World Report*, September 12, 1983.

Furniss, Tim, "Gulf Spy Sats." *Space*, November-December 1990.

Gertz, Bill, "Eavesdropping Complex in Cuba Being Upgraded." *Washington Times*, April 5, 1990.

Gilmartin, Patricia A., "France's Spot Satellite Images Helped U.S. Air Force Rehearse Gulf War Missions." *Aviation Week & Space Technology*, July 1, 1991.

Goodman, Glenn W., Jr., "From the Boardroom: Thomas V. Murphy." *Armed Forces Journal International*, July 1991.

"Gulf War Experience Sparks Review of RPV Priorities." *Aviation Week & Space Technology*, April 22, 1991.

Heller, Jean, "Photos Don't Show Buildup." *St. Petersburg Times* (Florida), January 6, 1991.

Hersh, Seymour M., "Target Qaddafi." *New York Times Magazine*, February 22, 1987.

Hotz, Robert, " 'Kelly' Johnson's Tour de Force." *Aviation Week & Space Technology*, March 9, 1964.

"In the Dead of the Night." *Time*, April 28, 1986.

Isaacson, Walter, "Nightstalkers in the Pacific Sky." *Time*, September 19, 1983.

"IZVESTIYA Investigates 1983 Downing of KAL 007." *Izvestiya*, January-February 1991.

Johnson, Clarence L., "Development of the Lockheed SR-71 Blackbird." *Lockheed Horizons*, Winter 1981/82.

Karch, Col. Lawrence G., "Very Low Cost UAVs." *Marine Corps Gazette*, March 1991.

"Kelly Johnson, Founder of 'Skunk Works,' Dies." *Aviation Week & Space Technology*, January 7, 1991.

Lake, Rear Adm. Julian S., "Despite Initial Problems, EW Systems Prove Effective in Desert Storm." *Armed Forces Journal International*, July 1991.

"Landsat Images Document Devastation of Oil Fields." *Aviation Week & Space Technology*, May 6, 1991.

Lerner, Preston, "Eye Spy." *California* magazine, August 1990.

Libbey, Miles A., III, and Maj. Patrick A. Putignano, "See Deep: Shoot Deep." *Military Review*, February 1991.

Marcus, Daniel J., "Bringing Images Down to EARTH." *Signal*, September 1986.

"Marines Test AeroVironment's Pointer Man-Portable RPV." *Aviation Week & Space Technology*, August 22, 1988.

Marshall, Eliot, "The Blackbird's Wake." *Air & Space*, October/November 1990.

Mathews, Tom:
"The Road to War." *Newsweek*, January 28, 1991.
"The Secret History of the War." *Newsweek*, March 18, 1991.

Narvaez, Alfonso A., "Clarence Johnson Is Dead at 80." *New York Times*, December 22, 1990.

"A New Kind of War." *Newsweek*, April 28, 1986.

"A New War—and New Risks." *U.S. News & World Report*, April 28, 1986.

Pappas, Terry, "The Blackbird Is Back." *Popular Mechanics*, June 1991.

Perry, Nancy J., "America's Arsenal." *Fortune*, February 25, 1991.

Pocha, J. J., and Ian Parker, "Understanding Orbital Dynamics." *Space*, March-April 1991.

Rawles, James W.:
"Commercial Imaging Comes Down to Earth." *Defense Electronics*, April 1989.
"A Voice in the Wilderness." *Defense Electronics*, August 1988.

"Reagan's Raiders." *Newsweek*, April 28, 1986.

Rhodes, Jeffrey P., "Aerospace World." *Air Force*, February 1990.

Richelson, Jeffrey T.:
"Air Force Tries to Shoot Down Its Own Spy." *Los Angeles Times*, April 9, 1989.
"The Future of Space Reconnaissance." *Scientific American*, January 1991.

Roos, John G.:
"SPOT Images Helped Allies Hit Targets in Downtown Baghdad." *Armed Forces Journal International*, May 1991.
"SPOT's 'Open Skies' Policy Was Early Casualty of Mideast Conflict." *Armed Forces Journal International*, April 1991.

Ropelewski, Robert R., "SR-71 Impressive in High-Speed Regime." *Aviation Week & Space Technology*, May 18, 1981.

"Satellite First of a Class of Spies for All Weather." *New York Times*, December 4, 1988.

Sawyer, Kathy, "U.S. Spies in the Sky Focus In on Iraqis." *Washington Post*, November 25, 1990.

Scarborough, Rowan:
"Aardvark Bites Mad Dog." *Defense Week*, April 21, 1986.
"Blackbird Flies into Retirement amid Oohs, Ahs, and Boos." *Washington Times*, March 7, 1990.

Scott, William B., "Companies Testing Long-EZ Derivative for Unmanned Aerial Vehicle Market." *Aviation Week & Space Technology*, April 27, 1987.

Shaker, Steven M., "Rotorplane RPVs." *National Defense*, July/August 1986.

Shapiro, Walter, "A Space Spy Gap." *Newsweek*, April 28, 1986.

Sloyan, Patrick J., "Spies in the Sky." *Washington Post*, February 25, 1990.

Smith, Bruce A., "U-2/TR-1s Provided Critical Data to Theater Commanders." *Aviation Week & Space Technology*, August 19, 1991.

"SR-71 Imposes Burden on Maintenance Units." *Aviation Week & Space Technology*, May 18, 1981.

Starr, Barbara, "Satellites Paved Way to Victory." *Jane's Defence Weekly*, March 9, 1991.

"Strategic Air Command to Form New Training Unit." *Aviation Week & Space Technology*, June 16, 1980.

Streetly, Martin, "US Airborne ELINT Systems Part 2: The U.S. Air Force." *Jane's Defence Weekly*, February 16, 1985.

Stumpf, Lt. Comdr. Robert E., "Air War with Libya." *U.S. Naval Institute Proceedings*, August 1986.

Sweetman, Bill, "Pointer and Cypher: Eyes over the Hill." *International Defense Review*, July 1990.

"Targeting a 'Mad Dog.'" *Newsweek*, April 21, 1986.

"Targeting Gaddafi." *Time*, April 21, 1986.

Tsipis, Kosta, "Arms Control Pacts Can Be Verified." *Discover*, April 1987.

Tyler, Patrick, "SR-71 Plane Roars into Retirement." *Washington Post*, March 7, 1990.

"Unarmed Jet Claims War's First Kill." *Stars and Stripes*, February 23, 1991.

"U.S. Demonstrates Advanced Weapons Technology in Libya." *Aviation Week & Space Technology*, April 21, 1986.

"The U.S. Strike against Libya." *Army Quarterly and Defense Journal*, April 1986.

"Washington Whispers." *U.S. News & World Report*, March 9, 1987.

Whitaker, Mark, "Inquest on a Massacre." *Newsweek*, September 19, 1983.

Wines, Michael, "Gulf Intelligence Draws Complaint by Schwarzkopf." *New York Times*, June 13, 1991.

OTHER SOURCES

"Blackbird's Swan Song Busts Records on Final Coast-to-Coast Run." Press Release. West Palm Beach, Fla.: United Technologies, Pratt & Whitney, March 6, 1990.

Campbell, David H.:
"F-12 Inlet Development." Conference Paper. Warrendale, Pa.: Society of Automotive Engineers, Inc., 1974.
"F-12 Series Aircraft Propulsion System Performance and Development." Conference Paper. New York: American Institute of Aeronautics and Astronautics, 1973.

"Coast to Coast in 68 Minutes." Press Release. Washington, D.C.: National Aeronautic Association, March 6, 1990.

Davies, Merton E., and William R. Harris, "RAND's Role in the Evolution of Balloon and Satellite Observation Systems and Related U.S. Space Technology." Paperback Document. Santa Monica, Calif.: The RAND Corp., September 1988.

Ford, J. P., et al., "Spaceborne Radar Observations." Pamphlet. Pasadena, Calif.: California Institute of Technology, Jet Propulsion Laboratory, December 15, 1989.

Green, S. Sgt. Daryl E., "1,000 Hours." Press Release. Beale AFB, Calif., September 9, 1983.

Johnson, Clarence L., "Some Development Aspects of the YF-12A Interceptor Aircraft." Conference Paper. New York: American Institute of Aeronautics and Astronautics, 1969.

"Lockheed TR-1 Reconnaissance Aircraft." Fact Sheet. Burbank, Calif.: Lockheed-California Company, January 1985.

McMaster, John R., and Frederick L. Schenk, "The Development of the F-12 Series Aircraft Manual and Automatic Flight Control System." Conference Paper. New York: American Institute of Aeronautics and Astronautics, 1973.

Miller, Jay, "Lockheed SR-71 (A-12/YF-12/D-21)." Brochure. Austin, Tex.: Aerofax, Inc., 1983.

Miller, Richmond L., Jr., "Flight Testing the F-12 Series Aircraft." Conference Paper. New York: American Institute of Aeronautics and Astronautics, 1973.

"150-mm Optical Bar Panoramic Camera PC-150A." Brochure. Lexington, Mass.: Itek Optical Systems, no date.

Rich, Ben. Speech given on January 26, 1990, at SR-71 Retirement Ceremony at Beale AFB, Calif.

Rich, Ben R., "The F-12 Series Aircraft Aerodynamic and Thermodynamic Design in Retrospect." Conference Paper. New York: American Institute of Aeronautics and Astronautics, 1973.

"72-Inch LOROP Panoramic Camera PC-202." Brochure. Lexington, Mass.: Itek Optical Systems, no date.

"SR-71." Fact Sheet. Beale AFB, Calif., June 1988.

"USAF/Lockheed SR-71 Advanced Reconnaissance Aircraft." Brochure. Burbank, Calif.: Lockheed Aeronautical Systems Co., July 24, 1986.

Wright, Sgt. Renee, "SR-71 Pioneer Recalls Days of Mach 3." Press Release. March AFB, Calif., February 28, 1990.

Index

Picture Credits

The sources for the illustrations that appear in this book are listed below. Credits from left to right are separated by semicolons; from top to bottom they are separated by dashes.
Cover: U.S. Navy, K-123742. 6: Image and elevation data courtesy © CNES, 1991, SPOT Image Corporation, and STX Remote Sensing Services. Photograph courtesy Visual Information Technologies, Inc. 8, 9: Sojuzkarta, USSR. 10-13: Image and elevation data courtesy © CNES, 1991, SPOT Image Corporation, and STX Remote Sensing Services. Photograph courtesy Visual Information Technologies, Inc. 14: Catherine LeRoy/Sipa Press. 16: Noel-Figaro/Gamma Liaison. 19: UPI/Bettmann. 23: Department of Defense/Scott Davis. 24: Department of Defense (2). 26, 27: George Hall/Check Six. 29: Charlie Cole/Picture Group, Inc. 31: Brian Shul/Mach I, Inc. 33: John Gaffney/Mach I, Inc. 34, 35: Dino Corbin/Mach I, Inc. 36: Sojuzkarta, USSR. 40, 41: U.S. Air Force. 42, 43: U.S. Air Force, courtesy General James Brickel. 44, 45: Office of U.S. Air Force History; U.S. Air Force. 48, 49: Courtesy Time Inc. Magazine Picture Collection. 50, 51: AP/Wide World. 52-55: Lockheed, Sunland, Calif. 61: *Aviation Week & Space Technology*;

National Archives, 342-K-25265. 64, 65: AP/Wide World. 67: Private collection. 68, 69: Art by Stephen R. Wagner (2), inset art, p.68, by Time-Life Books; MacDonald Dettwiler & Associates. 70: MacDonald Dettwiler & Associates. 74, 75: NASA. 76, 77: U.S. Geological Survey, Flagstaff, Ariz. 78, 79: Autometric, Inc. (5). 80, 81: Image and elevation data courtesy © CNES, 1991, SPOT Image Corporation, and STX Remote Sensing Services. Photograph courtesy Visual Information Technologies, Inc. (3). 82, 83: Visual Information Technologies, Inc. (7). 84, 85: Image and elevation data courtesy © CNES, 1991, SPOT Image Corporation, and STX Remote Sensing Services. Photograph courtesy Visual Information Technologies, Inc. (2). 86: Naval Weapons Center, China Lake, Calif. 90: Courtesy Time Inc. Magazine Picture Collection. 95: Association of Old Crows, Alexandria, Va. 98, 99: Robert S. Hopkins III. 101: Department of Defense, DF-ST-82-00951. 102, 103: AP/Wide World. 104, 105: Department of Defense, DN-ST-89-06435.

106: U.S. Navy, K-123742—Aerospace Publishing Ltd., London. 109: Courtesy Eshel Dramit Ltd. 110, 111: Courtesy Jeffrey Richelson. 113: *Aviation Week & Space Technology.* 114, 115: Art by Stephen R. Wagner. 118, 119: Courtesy California Microwave, Woodland Hills, Calif. 120, 121: Aerovironment, Inc. 122, 123: Israel Aircraft Industries International Inc.—AAI Corporation; Department of Defense, DN-ST-87-04512. 124, 125: Canadair Challenger, Inc. (3). 126: David Freese, inset George C. Marshall Foundation, Lexington, Va. 130, 131: A. Roux/Explorer, Paris. 132, 133: Art by Fred Holz. 134, 135: Hans Halberstadt/Arms Communications. 136, 137: Department of Defense, DN-SN-90-01835. 138: Hans Halberstadt/Arms Communications. 139: David Freese. 140: AP/Wide World—Time Inc. Magazine Picture Collection. 142, 143: Hans Halberstadt/Arms Communications. 144, 145: AP/Wide World. 146, 147: U.S. Air Force. 149: Martin Marietta, Denver. 151: Private collection. 152: Department of Defense.

TIME ® **LIFE** BOOKS

Time-Life Books
is a division of Time Life Inc.,
a wholly owned subsidiary of
THE TIME INC. BOOK COMPANY

TIME-LIFE BOOKS

PRESIDENT: Mary N. Davis

MANAGING EDITOR: Thomas H. Flaherty
Director of Editorial Resources: Elise D. Ritter-Clough
Director of Photography and Research:
John Conrad Weiser
Editorial Board: Dale M. Brown, Roberta Conlan, Laura Foreman, Lee Hassig, Jim Hicks, Blaine Marshall, Rita Thievon Mullin, Henry Woodhead
Assistant Director of Editorial Resources/Training Manager:
Norma E. Shaw

PUBLISHER: Robert H. Smith

Associate Publisher: Ann M. Mirabito
Editorial Director: Russell B. Adams, Jr.
Marketing Director: Anne C. Everhart
Production Manager: Prudence G. Harris
Supervisor of Quality Control: James King

Editorial Operations
Production: Celia Beattie
Library: Louise D. Forstall
Computer Composition: Deborah G. Tait (Manager), Monika D. Thayer, Janet Barnes Syring, Lillian Daniels
Interactive Media Specialist: Patti H. Cass

Correspondents: Elisabeth Kraemer-Singh (Bonn); Christine Hinze (London); Christina Lieberman (New York); Maria Vincenza Aloisi (Paris); Ann Natanson (Rome). Valuable assistance was also provided by Mehmet Ali Kislali (Ankara), Nihal Tamraz (Cairo), Marlin Levin and Jean Max (Jerusalem), Elizabeth Brown and Katheryn White (New York), Ann Wise (Rome), Mieko Ikeda (Tokyo).

THE NEW FACE OF WAR

SERIES EDITOR: Lee Hassig
Series Administrator: Judith W. Shanks

Editorial Staff for *Electronic Spies*
Art Director: Christopher M. Register
Picture Editor: Charlotte Marine Fullerton
Text Editor: Stephen G. Hyslop
Senior Writer: James M. Lynch
Associate Editors/Research: Mark G. Lazen (principal), Robin Currie, Susan M. Klemens
Writer: Charles J. Hagner
Assistant Art Director: Brook Mowrey
Senior Copy Coordinators: Anthony K. Pordes (principal), Elizabeth Graham
Picture Coordinator: David Beard
Editorial Assistant: Kathleen S. Walton

Special Contributors: George Constable, Ken Croswell, George Daniels, Jim Dawson, John DeMott, Lee Ewing, Tim Kelley, Tom Logsdon, Craig Roberts, T. J. Sodroski, Diane Ullius (text); Vilasini Balakrishnan, Douglas Brown, Catherine Halesky, John Leigh, Sheila K. Lenihan, Louis Plummer, Barbara Jones Smith, Susan Sonnesyn, Joann S. Stern (research); Mel Ingber (index).

Library of Congress Cataloging in Publication Data
Electronic spies/by the editors of Time-Life Books.
   p. cm. (The New face of war).
   Includes bibliographical references and index.
   ISBN 0-8094-8620-2
   1. Electronic intelligence. I. Time-Life Books. II. Series.
UG485.E52 1991
623.7'34—dc20   91-10296 CIP
ISBN 0-8094-8621-0 (lib. bdg.)